The End of Unbelief

"This is an unusual, deeply felt, utterly logical, and persuasive book—persuasive for its lucid arguments and its allowing the agnostic his or her helplessness in the absence of the material proof of God's existence. But *The End of Unbelief* is important for its combination of shrewd philosophical argument with heart, and that's why I intend to keep it near and go on pondering it. An excellent contribution to the great theological debate."

> —**Paul Theroux**, prominent travel writer and author of forty-six books, including *Ghost Train to the Eastern Star, Dark Star Safari*, and *Mosquito Coast*

"This book makes the question of God come alive and real in a way that no purely academic work can equal. Its raw spiritual insight and autobiographical frankness will grab hold of you and keep your attention no matter what your beliefs may be. Highly recommended."

> —**John F. Haught**, senior fellow in science and religion at Woodstock Theological Center, Georgetown University, and author of eighteen books, including *God and the New Atheism*

"If you're looking for an intelligent response to the growing number of agnostics and atheists whose books are on the shelves of almost every bookstore, and whose arguments are broadcast on television and radio talk shows day in and day out, you will find one in Shane Hayes's book. This somewhat autobiographical account of his journey from skepticism to faith will not only bolster the beliefs of Christians but also will offer bona fide challenges to those who struggle with reasons to believe in the God of the Bible."

> —**Tony Campolo**, PhD, professor emeritus, Eastern University, and author of more than thirty books, including *Red Letter Christians: A Citizen's Guide to Faith and Politics* and *Choose Love Not Power: How to Right the World's Wrongs from a Place of Weakness*

"As a personal history of an intellectual and theological journey, Shane Hayes's *The End of Unbelief* is a highly readable narrative full of energy and 'agony' (in the Greek sense of 'agon' as in *Samson Agonistes*). His experience is often moving, and his arguments erudite, and carefully reasoned, even though, as an avowed atheist, I am not finally compelled to share the choice of belief with which his journey ends."

—**Thomas H. Blackburn,** centennial professor emeritus of English literature, Swarthmore College

"Given the spate of pro-atheist works that have appeared in recent times, this book should be most welcome and refreshing for many serious readers. Hayes advances his argument in a highly personal, novel, varied, and very often eloquent fashion. An intellectually stimulating and enjoyable read."

—**Daniel J. Ziegler,** PhD, former dean, Graduate School of Arts and Sciences, and currently professor emeritus of psychology, Villanova University

"A fresh approach to an old issue. What Hayes calls agnosticism and skepticism lead him to a strong conclusion that you can have faith without accepting all the common explanations and assumptions that cling to words like *God* and *faith*. Using personal experience and reasoned reflections in a way most readers will understand, he provides a clear, persuasive reminder of the true stakes in these questions."

—**Anthony Battaglia,** professor emeritus of religious studies, California State University, Long Beach

THE END OF UNBELIEF

To Matthieu & Stephanie,
Best wishes and
warm regards.
   Shane Hayes.
   11·15·2014
P.S. Matt, thank you for
setting up my first blog,
which produced Part One
of this book.

THE END OF UNBELIEF

a new approach to the question of God

ARGUMENTS & STORIES BY THE ^{former} ATHEIST

S H A N E H A Y E S

LEAFWOOD
P U B L I S H E R S
an imprint of Abilene Christian University Press

THE END OF UNBELIEF
a new approach to the question of God

LEAFWOOD
P U B L I S H E R S
an imprint of Abilene Christian University Press

Copyright © 2014 by Shane Hayes

ISBN 978-0-89112-438-2 | LCCN 2014015750
Printed in the United States of America

Scripture quotations, unless otherwise noted, are from the Revised Standard Version of
the Bible, copyright © 1946, 1952, and 1971 the Division of Christian Education of the
National Council of the Churches of Christ in the United States of America. Used by
permission. All rights reserved.

Scripture quotations noted KJV are from the King James Version of the Bible.

Published in association with the Seymour Agency, 475 Miner Street Road,
Canton, NY 13617.

LIBRARY OF CONGRESS CATALOGING-IN-PUBLICATION DATA
Hayes, Shane, 1938-
  The end of unbelief : a new approach to the question of God : arguments & stories / by
the former atheist Shane Hayes.
    pages cm
  Includes bibliographical references.
  ISBN 978-0-89112-438-2
  1. Christianity and atheism. 2. Apologetics. 3. Conversion--Christianity. I. Title.
  BR128.A8H39 2014
  239--dc23
                                                                    2014015750

Cover design by Elizabeth Fulton
Interior text design by Sandy Armstrong, Strong Design

All contact with Shane Hayes should be sent by email to shanehayes@comcast.net, or
by regular mail to Shane Hayes c/o Leafwood Publishers.

Leafwood Publishers is an imprint of Abilene Christian University Press
1626 Campus Court, Abilene, Texas 79601
1-877-816-4455 | www.leafwoodpublishers.com
                14 15 16 17 18 19 / 7 6 5 4 3 2 1

This book is lovingly dedicated to

Peter and Anne, my parents,
to Mary Ellen, my wife,
and to my children,
Robin, Christian, Holly, and Candace

Acknowledgments

For intelligent reader reactions and editorial help, I have many to thank: my wife, Mary Ellen, whose support and inspiration transcend the literary; my daughters, Robin, Holly, and Candace; my son, Chris; Bill Rayner; Joe and Regina Petrecca; Bill Andiario; Ken DeCarlo; Jack Curran; Pete Krok; Anthony Mazzone; Volney James, formerly an editor at Biblica; Mary Sue Seymour, my agent for this book; Gary Myers, my acquisitions editor at Leafwood; and Mary Hardegree, Leafwood's managing editor.

I am deeply indebted to those who generously read and endorsed this book long before I was a published author with any claim to their time or attention: Paul Theroux, gifted novelist and possibly the most famous travel writer in the world; Professor John F. Haught of Georgetown University; Professor Daniel J. Ziegler of Villanova University; Professor Tony Campolo of Eastern University; Professor Thomas H. Blackburn of Swarthmore College; and Professor Anthony Battaglia of California State University, Long Beach. Their praise gave an unpublished author and his book a credibility that made all the difference.

Contents

"If there is a God, his methods are very subtle."
—Ronald Pavone

"How unsearchable are his judgments and how inscrutable his ways!"
—Romans 11:33b

"Man is born to trouble as the sparks fly upward."

—Job 5:7

Introduction

*T*his book has five discrete units, written at different periods of my life over half a century. All deal with the question of God's existence and the profound impact of belief or unbelief on a human life.

Part One is pure argument. It takes on the New Atheism, showing that it is a belief system, not a proven theory, and that it offers less to rational thinkers than faith in God does.

Part Two is a memoir told in fictional form. It tells how a fiercely ardent Catholic faith caused a crisis in my life at seventeen (I nearly entered a Trappist monastery) and how it was resolved. The influence of Thomas Merton, the famous Trappist monk and author, was central to the conflict. I include a sketch of the man and our meeting in the story.

Part Three is a blend of argument and memoir. It describes my passage through atheism, Hinduism, and Buddhism, to Pure Theism—which I describe in Part One—and finally back to Christianity. I dramatize and debate the problem of evil in a courtroom scene with God as defendant.

Part Four narrates a believer's last and finest hour.

Part Five shows how one who is philosophically agnostic yet passionately Christian sees the life and mission of Christ.

Part 1

An Agnostic and a Believer
(You Can Be Both)

Darkness
and Light

We are nocturnal creatures. Darkness is our element. The future is shrouded in deep mist and shadow. We can't see very clearly and we can't see very far, so we feel our way, grope, and guess at what's ahead. Faith is our candle, flickering, dim, uncertain, but necessary. Faith in science, faith in our intuitions and calculations, faith in luck, faith in God. There are many kinds of faith. We live by one or more of them. Without it we weaken, we fall, we perish.

Not only Scripture but all of human experience tells us we need something strong, good, and wise to believe in. For some, it's a statue of Zeus or Sophia; for some, kinetic theory and the empirical method; for some, the writings of a brilliant atheist; for some, Confucius, Buddha, Allah, the God of Abraham, or (for me) Christ. To believe is to hold as true what cannot yet be verified. It's a conviction, a sense of direction, that helps us move bravely through our darkness. And face what lies beyond it—the blackness of utter extinction or endless light.

chapter 1

An Agnostic Argues for Faith

In 2004, *The End of Faith* by Sam Harris becomes an international bestseller. The New Atheism soon is trumpeted by other eloquent voices: Dawkins (*The God Delusion*), Hitchens (*God Is Not Great*), Dennett (*Breaking the Spell*), and Stenger (*God: The Failed Hypothesis*). Essays proclaiming there are no good arguments for God's existence appear on op-ed pages of large metropolitan dailies. Three close friends surround me after dinner and declare that Christians give only inane reasons for believing in God in the face of human suffering and tragedy.

The tide of modern intellectual culture flows strongly toward atheism, a destination congenial to some but abhorrent to others. For me, it was like Antarctica—glacially cold and wind lashed, an icebound waste devoid of tree, shrub, or flower, no hint of blossoming life visible on the horizon, and beyond the horizon . . . *nothing*. I endured my own atheism for most of a decade. Then, drawn homeward, I swam against the tide for years, made a grueling journey back to the island of faith—for me, a lush Capri of the soul. Drifting with the tide is pleasant and easy, but is atheism where you want to go? Or stay?

What "Agnostic" Really Means

I am a Christian. And I am an agnostic. I hold as true what cannot yet be verified. An agnostic is one who says we can't *know* whether there is a God or not. His existence can't be proven, and it can't be disproven. Thomas Aquinas gave reasons to believe in God. I see the best of them as strong arguments, but not proofs. Bertrand Russell, a great proponent of atheism, admitted he couldn't be absolutely sure God doesn't exist. Chapter 4 of Dawkins's book is entitled "Why There Is Almost Certainly No God." *Almost* certainly. Dawkins isn't sure, either.

Since none of us can *know*, the great question isn't "to be or not to be," but to believe or not to believe. I believe. Atheists choose not to believe. I can't tell them they're wrong, and they can't tell me I'm wrong. We all grope in existential darkness. I use religious faith as a compass. They think it's worthless.

I don't say everyone should believe as I do. I'm a pragmatist, not an evangelist. I know how *different* people are. My solution may not be yours. But of this I'm sure: believing in God can enrich the lives of many who have ignored or rejected that option.

The Way Out of Our Maze

We're in this mess together—we're all human, vulnerable to illness, crushing accidents, the carnage of war, calamities of every kind. We're aging, and we're mortal. We don't know whether there's an all-powerful God who cares deeply about his creatures, or not. There is reason to think there is not. There is reason to think there is. Either hypothesis seems far-fetched in light of certain observable facts. From six-day creation, to creation over eons with evolution, to cosmic inflation, to the Big Bang theory, there is no explanation of the universe that is not from some point of view wildly improbable.

So we must have either no explanation or an unlikely one. To some rational minds, the theistic view is less unlikely than the atheistic. Did the Big Bang ultimately produce Einstein, or did a cause more like Einstein produce him? Did cosmic dust evolve into a great mind, or did a Great Mind produce the cosmos? Since the keenest powers of human reasoning leave us without proof on this crucial issue, uncertainty is our fate. We can't *know*. We can only *believe*.

But the atheist says, "I *don't* believe." Ahh, but you do, I reply. You don't believe in God, but you believe in No God. You believe in the hypothesis that there is no God. I believe in the hypothesis that there is a God. Mine is a religious belief; yours an unreligious belief. But we both believe. Some atheists would rather die than admit this.

Questions We Can't Escape

I can't say with certainty that there is a God. But I can say with certainty that *if* there is a God, that reality makes a huge difference in the character of the universe and of human life. Consider these three questions that we can't escape, because they keep coming at us:

1. When faced with problems or troubles that seem overwhelming, is supernatural help available or not?

2. Are we ephemeral creatures who expire utterly with our last breath, or is there a spirit in us that survives physical death?

3. If death is not the end of human consciousness, if there is a whole realm of being beyond that, is it good or bad—or might it be *either*, depending on how we relate to each other and how we relate to God . . . *while we're here*?

Atheists have decided that there is no supernatural help and death ends all. Fine, but that belief has consequences. The world feels different because they view it in that light. If supernatural help is available only to those who reach out for it in faith, they won't get that help. The joy of feeling the presence of a loving God in their lives, and connecting with him in prayer, will never be theirs. Thoughts of our mortality are more daunting if we can't link them to thoughts of our immortality. Grief is blacker if the lost child, parent, friend, or lover is gone forever, not just gone ahead. And if this life is harder because we have rejected belief in God, a future life might be harder still because we've done so.

Somber or Radiant?

These are a few ways in which faith can enrich people's lives and its rejection can impoverish them. Since we can't know whether the world is godless or God-filled, why not embrace the *radiant* view and enjoy its benefits? Why not swim against the tide?

chapter 2

Believing without Proof

"You can't be both a believer in God and an agnostic," I am told.

"Well then," I reply, "which am I *not*? Because I think I'm both. I believe in a personal God who created the world and cares about his creatures, and I pray to him daily—often hourly. Am I not a believer?"

"If you say so, I guess you are. But then you're not an agnostic."

There, I think, is the nub of the dispute. Most people think an agnostic is one who does not believe in God. And most people who call themselves agnostics probably don't. But agnosticism per se does not exclude belief. The *Oxford English Dictionary* (OED) defines "agnostic" as a "person who holds the view that nothing can be known of the existence of God or of anything beyond material phenomena."

"Agnostic" Does Not Mean "Unbeliever"

Here's my simple working definition: "An agnostic is one who says we can't know whether there is a God or not. His existence can't be proven, and it can't be disproven." I call this philosophical agnosticism, and it does not conflict with the more formal language, above. To state, as the OED does, that nothing can be *known* of the existence of God is not to say God doesn't exist. It speaks of the limits of our knowledge, not the limits of reality.

The OED gives eleven definitions of "know." For us, the one most on point—and most revealing—is the tenth: "Comprehend as fact or truth; understand with clearness and certainty. Freq[uently]. opp[osed to]. *Believe*." To *know* is to have certainty, and that's often seen as the opposite of *believing*. To say we can't know of the existence of God makes me an agnostic. But I *believe* in it—very strongly. There is no conflict between philosophical agnosticism and theistic belief.

Philosophical Position

We're not just parsing words here; we're touching on the complexity of human nature and a distinction (almost a dichotomy) that even philosophers often miss. We are multifaceted creatures. When my rational mind—after utmost exertion—concludes that we can't *know* whether there is a God or not, that his existence can't be either proven or disproven, my mind has done all it can. *In terms of philosophical position,* I'm an agnostic.

Personal Belief

But it doesn't end there, because I'm not a disembodied mind. I'm a human being with a physical, emotional, social, and—I submit—even a spiritual life. Here I am, on an obscure planet, adrift on the great sea of time, trying to figure out who and what I am and where I'm going, in the short term and the long term. And wondering if the long term ever ends. I have to move on. Get from here to there. Plot a course, form strategies, make assumptions, draw conclusions from limited evidence.

In evaluating my situation, mundane and cosmic, the question of whether God exists has profound relevance. Philosophy and science don't answer it. In that department, I'm an agnostic. But the imperatives of a reflective human life require that I *form an opinion* on what I can't know, and that I proceed as if there is a personal and loving God or as if there is not.

At age twenty, I came to believe that there was no God. That was my chosen creed. So I was an agnostic philosophically, and an atheist in personal belief. Years later, *without changing my philosophical position*, I embraced theism and later still, the Christian faith. So I am now an agnostic philosophically, and a Christian in personal belief. A believing agnostic.

Why "Agnostic" Is Misunderstood

The term "agnostic" is widely misunderstood because so many miss the distinction I've just made, between *personal agnosticism* and philosophical agnosticism. "I'm an agnostic" often means "I don't believe in God, but I don't *deny* his existence either, so I'm an agnostic, not an atheist." This is a loose, untidy use of the term "agnostic," which makes it hard to speak and think clearly about its philosophical meaning. That kind of unbeliever would do better to call himself *an uncommitted agnostic*, as distinguished from *a believing agnostic* like me, or *a disbelieving agnostic* whose personal creed is atheism.

Skeptics, Come as You Are

I proclaim this good news to atheists and uncommitted agnostics: You don't have to renounce a spirit of skepticism to believe in God. Agnostic philosophy lets you retain all your reasons for denying his existence. You needn't repudiate any of them. As long as you can discern this truth: even the strongest anti-God arguments are *not conclusive*, and the not-quite-disproven God may in fact be real; so, *you can hang on to agnosticism with one hand and grasp faith with the other.* I've done it and it works.

Proof-Claiming Theists

Do I contend that agnosticism is the only right philosophical view and that everyone, including Christians, Jews, and Muslims, should be philosophically agnostic? Here I'm a little inconsistent. I do hold that agnosticism is the most reasonable view. But if believers in God think they can prove his existence, I won't argue against them. I would be glad if they were right and I were wrong. I *will* argue against atheist claims that they can prove—or be sure—that God does not exist. As one who has chosen to believe, I have a strong bias in favor of the God hypothesis. I would not impose it on anyone, but I will defend its reasonableness against attacks.

Uncertainty and Faith

The last point I will make here is important, though not novel. The essence of believing is to hold as true what you cannot prove. The OED, in its nine definitions of "believe," uses such phrases as "have confidence or faith in . . . hold an opinion, think . . . give credence to . . . hold as true the existence of." All imply an element of uncertainty.

We don't *believe in* the existence of the house we live in. We know it's there; our senses confirm its reality. We don't *believe in* the law of gravity. We experience and deal with it all the time. I contend that we can't *believe in* God if God's existence is an absolute certainty. If that were so, we would be knowers, not believers, and our religion would be a body of knowledge, not *a faith*. In the Gospels, when Jesus urged people to believe, he was asking them to hold as true something unproven—often something that seemed incredible. That challenging fusion of belief with uncertainty is what makes faith a virtue. And it should make believers tolerant of philosophical agnosticism, even if they think God's existence as provable as gravity.

In *Dogmatics in Outline*, Karl Barth, the great theologian, said: "Note well: in the whole Bible of the Old and New testaments not the slightest attempt is ever made to *prove* God" (37). Barth saw God as "unprovable" and assured his Christian readers that "God has not the slightest need for our proofs" (38).

chapter 3

How the Improbable God Probably Works

(A Worldview and a God Hypothesis)

Here's a worldview in a thousand words—and it took me only fifty years to compose it. I offer it as a hypothesis—my effort to explain how God must think and act if we are to reconcile his existence with the world, and human life, as we find them. In part, they are speculations about the mind, the values, and—to use a crude term for want of a better one—the *personality* of God. (If he is a person, must he not have a personality, "the complex of characteristics that distinguishes an individual"?) Assume each part is true until you get to the end. Then, when you view it whole, decide if it might *possibly* account for what we see and what *may* be behind it. For me it does.

The Personality of God

There is a cosmic intelligence, an all-powerful personal God who created the universe. The Big Bang, evolution, and natural selection may have been his modus operandi. His mind is infinite, and *his methods are very subtle*. A sense of humor is one of the finest aspects of human intelligence, so we should not suppose our creator is without one. Irony and a predilection for the incongruous, the unexpected, the mysterious, and the imponderable are manifest in all his works.

He has made some of the greatest truths about his world—from the roundness of the earth, and the stillness of the sun, to his own invisible existence—appear improbable. He reveals himself, but always under a cloak of ambiguity that lets us explain him away, if we want to. He does this not maliciously, but with a benevolent purpose that has something to do with *freedom* and what might be called *soul making*. His heart is as vast and limitless as his mind.

Man is the creature in whom he takes the greatest interest, because man is the most Godlike creature—the most able to reflect on his condition and alter it by using his mind and his power of choice. Man is the only creature capable of knowing God and forming a relationship with him, the only creature with a sense of humor.

The Values of God

God loves all of his creation, especially man, and he has made man more capable of love than any other creature. Man can love not only himself, his mate, and their offspring (as other mammals do), but a wide circle of other human beings—potentially all of them. And God made it possible for man to love *him*. He has made love crucial to a healthy human psyche. We are happiest when we love God and other people, but we are free not to.

Such choices are the essence of morality, and God constructed the universe around them. Despite the vast sweep of its galaxies, it is essentially *a moral universe*—designed to provide moral challenge and opportunity, to require moral striving, and to produce in every life a measurable degree of moral success and failure, which are of keen interest to God.

Our happiness is important, but must often be deferred. God is eternal—he takes the long view, and requires that *we* learn to do so as well. The long view includes both life, which is brief, and its Sequel, which is endless. Though the Sequel is infinitely larger than life, it's as invisible as God, and therefore easy to forget or not believe in.

Deceptive Appearances, Hidden Truths

God has filled his universe with ironies. The principal irony is that often *things are not what they seem*. Learning to deal with that is a great moral challenge. We must learn to "see" the invisible, to "hear" the inaudible, to "grasp" what we can't touch, and to believe what we can't prove. The most important reality is God, but he's hidden from us. Deliberately, maddeningly, and distressingly hidden. The shining Sequel to life—its fulfillment, point, and purpose—is so out of sight as to be generally out of mind, even for those who expect it.

God has made it possible for man to know a great many things with certainty. We know obvious things by simple observation. Much that is hidden can be learned by study, experiment, and the exercise of reason. At its best, reason is so amazing that we're tempted to think it's the only human faculty that can lead us to truth. In fact, it can lead us to only certain kinds of truth: practical, theoretical, scientific. But the ultimate truth—interpersonal and mystical—is quite beyond its reach. We can reason to the *possibility* of God, but he has strewn other possibilities in our path, so that *certainty* about his existence and our origin cannot be had.

Unprovable, but Not Unreachable

Dealing with this uncertainty is another moral challenge. God has made himself not only hidden but unprovable. The only way to connect with him is by believing what we can't know. Those are his terms, and we must accept them or reject him. When reason brings us to God's threshold (seeing that he is one possibility among several), other faculties must carry us across, and if we disdain them, we'll never reach him. They may work in this sequence: Hope says, "I wish there were a God; I want there to be a God; I hope there is a God." Love says, "I find the idea of God wonderfully appealing; I love the idea of God; I love the possibility of God." Then faith says, "I extend my hand into the darkness; I believe in God"—and the divine connection is made!

Humility and Truth

The anonymous ancient mystic who wrote *The Cloud of Unknowing* said: "By love he may be gotten and holden, but by thought, never." The apostle John said, "God is love" (1 John 4:8). Atheist Bertrand Russell said, "Not enough evidence, God, not enough evidence," to justify his unbelief. Believing requires not only an act of faith but also an act of humility. The prouder we are of our intellect, of its superiority to lesser minds, and of the dazzling science it produced, the harder it is to humble ourselves and believe. Yet the designer of the universe arranged it so that he, his ultimate truth, and life's shining Sequel can be found only by the humble and believing.

We cannot accept his love unless we acknowledge his existence. We can brush aside the outstretched hand. He will neither compel faith nor make it unnecessary. On those terms, we can take him or leave him; receive his embrace or turn away. Our decision is our fate.

chapter 4

Do Billions Who Have Never Heard of God Prove There Is None?

A reader commented, rather eloquently, on Chapter Three when I posted it on my blog. I will refer to him hereafter simply as "C. S.," for challenging skeptic. I quote here part of what he said and then my response.

His Challenge

Shane:

You may care, and you may reach out to unbelievers, but you are not God. Reaching out always seems to require human agency. . . . [C. S. gives a list of the vast multitudes who were not reached by Saint Paul's missionary journeys, including over 100 million in China and on the Indian subcontinent. He also cites the "600 human generations ... before the ancient Hebrews decided there was only one god, and that they were his chosen people." He continues:]

The number of people to whom the Christian God failed to reach out runs into the tens of billions. Why? I have my theory—there was no God to do the reaching out. What's your theory? Why did the Christian God, who supposedly cares so profoundly that people believe that he exists, never bother to make known to so many the possibility of his existence?

My Response

C. S.:

Though I am a Christian, I am not a Christian apologist. Many can defend Christianity better than I, so I generally speak here as a Pure Theist. My reflections on the Christian God may be unorthodox, but I'll make a few as I argue the simpler case for *a caring, personal God*.

You're right; God usually works through human agents. But *he sometimes stirs the heart directly*. Though even Christians admit that the Argument from Universal Belief is not conclusive, its premise is relevant here: "It is generally true that every people or tribe of men has had some kind of belief in a supreme being" (*Catholic Encyclopedia*). Even you, C. S., might concede that the impulse to worship something greater than oneself has been widespread since the dawn of history and probably before. If the God of my hypothesis implanted such a need and urge in humankind, he would allow for its expression in forms appropriate to the knowledge, opportunity, and mental capacity of each of his creatures.

A Pagan Aboriginal

If a tenth-century Australian aboriginal never heard of Christ or Yahweh, her kneeling down, extending her arms skyward in grateful wonder, and worshipping the sun would, for her, be as pleasing to my pure-theistic God (and I believe to the Judeo-Christian God) as attendance at a solemn high Mass.

If she stayed awake for long weary hours cradling her sick child, administering a potion of boiled roots believed to be medicinal, and intoning primitive incantations to the sun on his behalf, divine wisdom would see her as having fulfilled Christ's two great commandments—to love God and love people—as admirably as Jairus, who implored Jesus directly on his daughter's behalf.

The caring God of my hypothesis is not indifferent to any human creature of any era. Nor does he demand of the most afflicted and isolated any more than their poor capacities and constricted circumstances allow them to *do, be,* or *believe.*

Blameless Ignorance

In judging moral culpability, church teaching contains the concept of "vincible and invincible ignorance" (ignorance that's our own fault and ignorance that we can't help). My tenth-century aboriginal was *invincibly ignorant* of everything proclaimed in the New Testament and therefore blameless for not believing in Jesus and his gospel. She felt innate promptings to acknowledge a being of superhuman power, somehow related to her life, and responded by worshipping the sun. Her mate may have resisted those same promptings, and been unwilling to bestir himself, or sacrifice any comfort, to succor the suffering child.

A kind and omniscient God could apply the two great commandments to *them*, in their era and cultural milieu, as wisely and justly as he could apply them to *me* when, at age twenty, after fourteen years of Christian education, I renounced all I had once believed and became an atheist.

The All-Embracing Arms

God thus conceived could have existed through all the ages of the Earth, in the vast expanse of global cultures you point to, and could have had loving interactions with each of those nameless billions who groped toward him in their darkness. Though their literal concept of God was *wrong*, the earnestness of their effort to worship and connect was *right*.

Homage to a golden calf, *by one who knew no better*, might have been seen by a compassionate God as a metaphor for worshipping him. And refusal to act on the worship impulse, by one who valued nothing *beyond himself*, might have been, in that time and culture, a metaphor for atheism. Was the One who inspired the Book of Genesis, whose Son called himself "the Lamb of God," incapable of seeing truth in a metaphor?

This same large-hearted, all-seeing God could have planned and implemented an Incarnation, a Crucifixion, and a Resurrection, without excluding any who lived before or after those events, from the ultimate beatitude of his love, unless they chose to exclude themselves. And those who exclude themselves, as I did, will feel persistent invitations—some silent, some quite audible—to return. He doesn't give up on us lightly. Every time we glance at him, he beckons.

chapter 5

Is God's Existence Improbable?

(Does Probability Matter?)

In our talks about the existence of God, my atheist friends nearly always say something to this effect: "My *feelings* have nothing to do with this. Yours clearly do, and you admit it. But mine don't. I just weigh the evidence and seek the truth."

Among several important things I can't prove but am convinced of is this: in deciding whether or not to believe in God, no one, on either side of the issue, is completely objective. Nor *should* one be, since the arguments are weighty on both sides, and neither side proves its case. Evidence and logic leave us dangling. In forming an opinion of what is unknowable, personal considerations become relevant, even determinative.

Where evidence is overwhelming, we should sweep our feelings aside. For example, the proposition that all men are mortal and doomed to die is unpleasant to contemplate. When we look at a mortally ill person, ravaged by disease, or a desiccated body at a viewing, the thought that their fate will inevitably be ours is grim and morbid. Yet every rational person *disregards his emotional preferences and believes* that gruesome truth. A mountain of historical evidence, actuaries, the obituary pages, and our own observation all confirm that death is the terminus of every human life.

But does human *consciousness* survive death, and if so, in what form? Now there is a question for which we have almost no observable evidence. True, the lifeless body shows no signs of consciousness and never will again. Neural science has discovered much about the connections among awareness, perception, reasoning, and various parts of the brain. Does the fact of those connections during life prove that consciousness apart from them is impossible after death?

Is our knowledge of *All That Is* so complete that there can be no dimension in which human consciousness exists unmoored to a body? Might that possibility depend on whether the material universe (whose existence science can't explain) had a *non*physical cause—an omnipotent mind outside the world who created it? If an infinite intelligence is the uncreated source and inventor of matter, himself independent of it, might he not want his human creatures to exist independent of it too, when their mortal, moral life has ended?

When Evidence Is Fragmentary

Here we move into a realm in which evidence is absent, ambiguous, or inconclusive, so answers must be conjectural—a combination of guesswork and surmise. Rationality cites facts and makes arguments but admits in the end: *I can't be sure.* Some shrug and leave it at that, taking no position, forming no opinion. But to move from indecision to belief in either direction, as most of us do, we must either flip a coin or weigh factors that are not purely rational. Though we hate to admit it, our *feelings* come into play—and they should.

"Not so," my atheist friend insists. "I base my conclusion on assessing the probabilities. That's a quantitative judgment that has nothing to do with emotion. God's existence is so *extremely improbable* that atheism is the only rational choice."

But how improbable is *the alternative* to God? Science admits it doesn't know how life began. The odds against spontaneous generation of life, by random events, are staggering. Not only must non-living chemical matter come alive, *it must just happen to contain the kind of DNA or RNA necessary to reproduce itself genetically.* Otherwise the extraordinary phenomenon would die with no offspring, no consequence. So *two* virtual miracles must occur *at once!*

All efforts to create the most rudimentary forms of life in a lab, under ideal conditions, beginning with Miller and Urey in 1953, have failed. Bill Bryson in his wide-ranging survey of scientific developments (*A Short History of Nearly Everything*) says this:

> Despite a half century of further study, we are no nearer to synthesizing life today than we were in 1953 and much further away from thinking we can. . . . The problem is proteins. . . . By all the laws of probability proteins shouldn't exist. . . . To make [the protein] collagen you need to arrange 1,055 amino acids in precisely the right sequence. But . . . you don't make it. It makes itself spontaneously, without direction, and this is where the unlikelihood comes in.

THE END OF UNBELIEF

The chances of a 1,055 sequence molecule like collagen spontaneously self-assembling are, frankly, nil. It just isn't going to happen. (287–88)

Monkeying Around with the Odds

A contrary view is expressed by atheist Richard Dawkins, who argues that because there are a billion billion planets in the universe, a billion-to-one shot—like dead chemicals springing to life—becomes a sure thing. The same kind of mathematical prestidigitation has produced "the infinite monkey theorem," which Wikipedia describes thus: "A hypothetical chimpanzee . . . hitting keys at random on a typewriter keyboard for an infinite amount of time will almost surely type a given text, such as the complete works of William Shakespeare." With this kind of mathematical wizardry to light our path, who needs faith? Or common sense?

So my friend, the coolly rational atheist (a brilliant guy, by the way), has no problem believing that spontaneous generation of life took place, despite a level of improbability that can hardly be quantified. He puts faith in mathematical theories that are prima facie farfetched and in no way explain how dead matter not only comes to life but does so with reproductive capacity and eventually, with no outside help, evolves the still more dazzling prodigy of *consciousness*. Yet he can't believe in God because God's existence is "too improbable."

Conclusion

The probability of God's existence is a legitimate question, which the uncertain must grapple with, and which will be a factor in reaching their conclusion. I would argue:

- In this context, probability is too nebulous to assign a percentage or a ratio to.
- Just as with God's existence itself, reasonable minds may differ on whether the greater probability is that he exists or that he does not. Both sides see the scales as tipping in their favor.
- One's feelings (preferences) enter into a probability assessment, just as inevitably as they do into the final decision about whether God exists. And that's fine, if we overcome our denial and admit it, at least to ourselves.

In pondering the probability issue in Chapter One, "An Agnostic Argues for Faith," I asked myself these two questions: *Did the Big Bang ultimately produce Einstein, or did a cause more like Einstein produce him? Did cosmic dust evolve into a great mind, or did a Great Mind produce the cosmos?* Viewed in that light, I think the case for God is stronger than the case against. But even if you think the case against is formidable, and God quite improbable, a small ray of rational hope that he exists is enough to make belief a legitimate choice. What seems unlikely, even *extremely* unlikely, sometimes proves to be true.

In the fifth century BC, the Greek philosopher Democritus said he believed the universe was composed of indivisible atoms and void. No one could see the atoms, so most people—including Plato and Aristotle—thought he was wrong. He had no way of proving his hypothesis. It seemed very unlikely to be true. Two thousand years later, it still seemed like fantasy to most educated people. Today that unverifiable, almost incredible, belief has been vindicated. The extremely unlikely was true.

The God hypothesis, even if you think it highly improbable, may also prove to be true. No one can prove it false. Here is where human considerations—like the benefits of belief versus the detriments of unbelief—can reasonably and prudently be taken into account.

chapter 6

The Greatest
Scientific Mind

The point of the last chapter is that the improbability argument cuts both ways. I don't claim that, because science has not accounted for the existence of life and consciousness, the God hypothesis must be true. I merely say *it is rational to embrace that hypothesis.* Creation by an intelligent being is no more improbable than life occurring by chemical accident, and to my mind, the former idea is more credible. The New Atheists talk as if they have an absolutely sure thing (Stenger and Harris) or a virtually sure thing (Dawkins), and that the pro-faith position is delusion. That attitude is arrogant, and that assessment of the probabilities so unbalanced as to convict them of the self-delusion they decry in believers.

Some accuse me of relying on gaps in scientific knowledge to prove there's a God (a "God-of-the-Gaps" argument). I'm an agnostic. I don't attempt proof. But I have the impudence to point out weaknesses in the case for God's *non*existence (despite the ire this arouses in New Atheists). I applaud science's efforts to fill in the gaps; most scientific advances improve the human condition. I'm pro-science. It's no threat to *my* faith.

God and Einstein

Even if every gap were filled, every scientific question answered, the philosophical conundrum would remain: Do these explanations merely tell us *how the cosmic intellect did its work*, or do they explain God away? Where did the infinitely dense "singularity" come from, the "point of zero volume" that exploded with a Big Bang at the birth of the universe? The singularity caused the Big Bang, but *what caused the singularity*?

A magic particle, smaller than an atom, that contained the whole universe. Did it simply spring into being, charged with *potentiality* so stupendous that all space and time, all matter and energy—all of natural and human history—were compressed in this invisible unmeasurable inexplicable *seed*? Is there a work of science fiction that rivals the imaginative genius of that plot premise? Are we to believe it had no author?

Can we seriously ascribe it to chemical randomness or blind chance? And if we can, is that the *best* theory? Is it more likely that some arcane *chemical quirk* caused the singularity and its infinite consequences, or that an immense intellect conceived these wonders and had the power to make them real in time and space? A chemical quirk, or a dazzling intellect? Which better explains things? (At moments like this, I confess, my agnosticism is shaken. But it will recover.)

Lemaitre—with help from Einstein, Friedmann, and Hubble—gave us the Big Bang theory, but he didn't give us the Big Bang. That required creativity of a higher order.

The God of my hypothesis is not the paper tiger—the intellectual primitive—atheists delight in attacking, based on a literal view of Genesis. The God I believe in has a scientific mind as superior to Newton's and Einstein's as theirs were to the Neanderthal. Which is greater, the mind that propounds grand theories, or the Mind that produced the mind—and the universe the theorizing mind explains? I don't pray to the God of the Gaps but to *the God of the Gestalt, the God of the Totality*. I can't prove him, but his existence is eminently credible. And highly probable.

The Sovereignty of Hope

A skeptic challenged me with this comment: "As for life after death, I wouldn't say that there's evidence against it, or that I have any meaningful way of assessing the probability of life after death. I would just say that generally before one believes in statement Z, we require more than a statement that no one has shown Z to be impossible—we generally require positive evidence for Z."

Even if there were no evidence of life after death (and there *is*), the *possibility* is so intriguing—it would make so *vast* a difference—that to hope for it is neither irrational nor unjustified. If true (and it well might be) think how it transforms our perception of ourselves, our universe, and our future!

I know of a writer who showed no evidence of talent, but *hoped* it was there, acted on unsubstantiated hope for decades, and finally saw it materialize. If he had not staked his future *on hope alone* as a starting point, it would never have been fulfilled. So with forming a view of the universe, of the origin and destiny of human life: clues of the divine abound; yet were there none, a real *possibility*, even without evidence, can justify hope. And *life with hope* is better than life without it.

chapter 7

Does Atheism Break Down Here?

In chapter 4 of *The God Delusion*, Richard Dawkins says, "[T]he designer hypothesis immediately raises the larger problem of who designed the designer. The whole problem we started out with was the problem of explaining statistical improbability. It is obviously no solution to postulate something even more improbable" (188).

In the margin beside that statement I wrote: "But can't we explain something complex and amazing (the play *Hamlet*) by pointing to a cause even *more* complex and amazing (Shakespeare)?"

In the same chapter, Dawkins says:

> To suggest that the first cause, the great unknown which
> is responsible for something existing instead of nothing,
> is a being capable of designing the universe and of talking
> to a million people simultaneously, is a total abdication of

the responsibility to find an explanation. It is . . . thought-denying skyhookery. (185)

Hiding Weakness with Rhetoric

Dawkins's is a rhetorically forceful statement; many are convinced by it. But if you examine it closely, it is not a refutation of the "first cause" argument—it is mere intellectual *name-calling* with no rational substance. Pasting the labels "abdication" and "skyhookery" on a solid argument that threatens his position shows how weak the position is and how illogically Dawkins, for all his brilliance, tries to hide such weakness.

To say the wondrous world could not have had a still more wondrous creator is to deny the obvious. An inventor is greater than his machine. DaVinci was greater than his paintings. To say the more wondrous Creator must have had a creator is simply untrue. The argument that a creator must have had a creator, who must have had a creator, who must have had a creator, etc., etc., ad infinitum, is to involve oneself in *an infinite regress*, which keeps begging the question and solves nothing.

A Rational Way Out–"First" Means Uncaused

The *only way out* of an infinite regress is to posit that it stops somewhere, and that the end-of-regress is the first cause of all that is, itself uncaused. Yes, there *could* have been a starting point, a Being that always existed, before time began. Whose intelligence and powers are not limited, as ours are, but are vast beyond imagining. Who created the universe and set it in motion, perhaps by making the singularity that exploded with a Big Bang, giving birth to the galaxies, our planet, life, evolution, and all of history, human and natural. That kind of an all-sufficient starting point in no way violates logic. In fact, logic *requires* it.

And, yes, the author had to be eternal, uncreated, uncaused, in order to *be* the first cause. But that's not natural, you may object. No, it's not. It's *super*natural. Without an uncaused supernatural starting point, you have an endless chain of secondary causes—and *common sense regurgitates an infinite regress*. Ergo . . . God.

You may, like Hawking and Stenger, prefer to think that the singularity popped out of nothing, that *nothing caused something*; that ultimately *nothing caused everything*. In *The Grand Design*, Hawking said: "Because there is a law like gravity, the universe can and will create itself from nothing. Spontaneous creation is the reason there is something rather than nothing, why the universe exists, why we exist. It is not necessary to invoke God . . ." (180).

Nothing caused everything. Would you call that a natural explanation—or a supernatural explanation? Or an *un*natural explanation? Whichever, can you seriously argue that *nothing* is more plausible than God? Maybe Hawking and I can agree on this statement, though we inflect it to have opposite meanings:

Nothing is more plausible than God.

Nothing!

Alpha and Omega: The Beginning and the End

Dawkins, again in chapter 4, says that "any God capable of designing a universe . . . tuned to lead to our evolution, must be a supremely complex and improbable entity who needs an even bigger explanation than the one he is supposed to provide" (176).

Again, that's flatly untrue. A supremely complex cosmic intelligence, existing from all eternity, does not require a bigger explanation—or *any* explanation. He cannot be explained: he simply *is*.

Nor does the first cause hypothesis "explain nothing" about the origin of the universe. In fact, it explains *everything*. It's the most adequate explanation there can be. *It's where the need for an explanation ends.* You may not like it. If you hate the idea of God you'll hate the argument. But don't say it explains nothing, and smear graffiti on it like "abdication" and "skyhook."

Help!

In fact, it's such a powerful and comprehensive argument, I'm not sure how we get around it. Is infinite regress the best we can do? Or is "the singularity just popped out of nothing" the best? Is there a real rebuttal? Help me! My agnosticism is tottering. This looks like a proof.

(After a pause . . . .) Forgive that outburst. I've calmed down and am willing to admit that the God hypothesis is not a proof. But it strikes me as so superior to competing explanations that no one, however modern and sophisticated, should blush to make it his worldview.

chapter. 8

Magic:
Divine and Human

A skeptical reader objected to this paragraph from the last chapter:

> A supremely complex cosmic intelligence, existing from all
> eternity, does not require a bigger explanation. Nor does it
> "explain nothing." In fact, it explains *everything* about the
> origin of the universe. It's the most adequate explanation
> there can be. *It's where the need for an explanation ends.*

The reader C. S. said: "I disagree. It does indeed explain nothing,
because the 'explanation' is, at bottom, 'It was magic.' Invoking
magic, and leaving it at that, is not an explanation."

Rhetoric versus Substance

First, we must separate rhetoric from substance. Belittling an
idea by expressing it in pejorative words is not genuine refutation. For example, on atheist websites I often see God referred to

as "the Sky Fairy." No one wants to admit he buys in to fairy tales, so poorly fortified theists may be nudged away from theism, and atheists who use the term feel less threatened by the substance of theistic arguments. This is not a high order of rational discourse.

Throwing the word "magic" at the first-cause argument is like calling God a Sky Fairy. It may be rhetorically effective, in a superficial way, but it clouds the issue without addressing its substance. Magic has a number of meanings associated with superstition, sorcery, casting spells, and trickery. No serious theist has any time for that. But Webster also gives this definition of magic: "an extraordinary power or influence seemingly from a supernatural source."

Creation and Mystery

Now, "magic" thus defined is compatible with rational discourse. The God I believe in, and hypothesize for this argument, is a nonmaterial being, which is to say *a spirit*, of immense intellect and power, able to conceive of our physical universe—a thing apart from himself—and then make it real in space and time. The universe, with its astounding variety, complexity, and inconceivable dimensions, may be seen as manifesting "an extraordinary power . . . seemingly from a supernatural source." To the extent that "magic" means wrought by supernatural power, beyond the reach or comprehension of man, yes, there is a magical quality to divine creation.

My reader argued further:

To have a genuine explanation, you need to be able to specify how the trick was performed. But this is precisely the kind of explanation that you not only cannot provide, but that you seem to think is rendered superfluous by invoking a "supremely complex intelligence, existing from all eternity."

He forgets that science is often unable to "specify how the trick was performed." Scientists don't know what caused the singularity to exist in such extreme densities or temperatures, or to detonate with a Big Bang when it did, 13.7 billion years ago. They can only speculate. Nor do they know how the singularity became imbued with the DNA, so to speak, the cosmic genetic map, that blossomed into our universe—and ourselves. That is shrouded in mystery, but the Big Bang is still deemed a valid *explanation*.

Is God an Explanation?

The *American Heritage Dictionary* gives this definition: "**explain**: 1. To make plain or comprehensible . . . 3. To offer reasons for; justify." The God hypothesis does *make the origin of the universe comprehensible*; more comprehensible, for me, than any other explanation I have heard. It does *offer reasons for* the existence of a material world, which once did not exist; as well as for the complex structure of the cosmos, the laws that govern it, and even of the atom. (That structure appears to be the work of a brilliant inventor, and in the God hypothesis, it *is*.)

The God hypothesis throws light on the purpose of the cosmos, of human consciousness, and of the human struggle to prevail over adversity and even death.

So the God hypothesis *is* an explanation as dictionaries define one. It is not a *scientific* explanation, which is the kind some atheists demand ("the mechanism by which the universe came to be"). It does not give a progression of mechanical details, because a transcendent Being is not accessible to the empirical method. He is beyond the probing techniques of science.

To the extent that he can be explained at all, it must be by non-empirical speculative disciplines like philosophy and theology. And no, they don't provide scientifically verifiable certainty. As a believing agnostic, I contend that on the ultimate questions such certainty cannot be had. Since we can't *know* what is true, we must take either no position or one that is in essence *an opinion*, which is to say, a *belief*. Theism is a belief. Atheism too is a belief.

The Only Rational Way Out

Unlike attacks on evolutionary theory, the first-cause argument aims not at weak links in the scientific chain, but at the foundation of all reality. It does not depend on the Big Bang theory being true. Aristotle toyed with a first-cause theory in the fourth century BC; Aquinas refined and solidified it in the thirteenth century AD. It applied equally to the geocentric theory of Ptolemy (d. 165 AD), to the heliocentric theory of Copernicus fourteen hundred years later, and to the "steady state" cosmological model that was eclipsed by Lemaitre's Big Bang hypothesis. I have applied it to the Big Bang theory because that is now the most widely accepted cosmological view.

If the Big Bang theory dies with a whimper, its successor will face the same dilemma: an infinite regress of secondary causes is the only alternative to a first cause—except for the preposterous new theory that the universe *popped out of nothing* in the natural course of things. Proponents of the God hypothesis say the world was created *from* nothing. Now atheists say it was created *by* nothing. They're right to this extent: When you look for a first cause that is not a divine intelligence you find . . . *nothing*.

chapter 9

Evidence of
a Creator God

My friend is deeply versed in the New Atheist literature that is so
in vogue among intellectuals. He states categorically: "There is no
evidence—*zero evidence*—that God exists or that he created the
universe." For a moment, I'm nonplussed. My mind draws a blank.
I have loads of arguments, but . . . *evidence*? What does he want,
footprints? Are there no clues?

Then the lawyer in me reflects: What is evidence? The *Oxford
English Dictionary* gives this definition: "evidence: 2. An indication,
a sign . . . 3. Facts or testimony in support of a conclusion, statement, or belief . . . b. something serving as proof." Evidence need
not be proof. In the matters we're examining, I see no evidence on
either side that rises to the level of proof. But "facts in support of a
conclusion or belief"—that we have.

A World of Evidence

To those who say there's no evidence of a creator-God I reply: *the universe itself is evidence*. Abundant, and in many ways highly convincing, evidence. It is a vast complex of facts that can be seen as supporting the belief that a cosmic mind exists. The appearance of *inventive thought* is everywhere in our universe, from the laws and patterns that govern the galaxies to the composition of matter.

If matter were simply a blob of undifferentiated clay, as it appears to the eye, it would be easier to suppose it just happened. But matter is composed of molecules, and molecules are composed of atoms. Even atoms are not simple—they resemble a small solar system. The planetary model describes electrons "orbiting" a nucleus at the center, composed of positively charged particles called protons and electrically neutral particles called neutrons.

And there are subatomic particles: muons, pions, hyperons, mesons, baryons, and tachyons, to name a few. And then there are *quarks*. They come in six varieties, known as *flavors*: up, down, charm, strange, top, and bottom. A proton is made of two up quarks and one down quark. Among the intrinsic properties of quarks are electric charge, color charge, spin, and mass.

The Miracle of Matter–and Mind

When I got to the level of *quarks* it hit me: the astoundingly complex structure of matter—which only brilliant scientists could discover and comprehend—is evidence of a mind whose ingenuity far exceeds the human, one whose intellective fingerprints are all over the world. Maybe "a blob of glup" just happened. But the elegant architecture of the invisibly fine—of the atomic and subatomic realm—is no accident. Natural selection does not explain it. There's no Darwinian challenge to it. It's simply *there*, and has been for fourteen billion years, since the dust settled after the Big Bang. One can't help but contemplate it with a wild surmise.

The intricacy of living matter is even more dazzling. The human body contains at least ten trillion (ten million million) cells. In the nucleus of *every cell* are chromosomes that contain DNA, capable of transferring inherited characteristics. The DNA molecule is shaped like a twisted ladder (the famed "double helix"). Chemical compounds called "base pairs" are the rungs of the ladder. They carry genetic information that determines the size and shape of our bodies, the contours of our faces, our health and strength, even our mental capacities. There are *three billion of these base pairs* in every human cell. Three billion! In a cell so minute, it is invisible to the naked eye.

To appreciate the arcane functions of base pairs in the double helix, we'd have to be molecular biologists. As laymen, we can marvel at a level of complexity that can be mathematically expressed—but not imagined. Who can say it's not evidence of an infinite creative mind? There are competing explanations, but can anyone be *sure* that one is wrong? No! No one—not Dawkins, or Harris, or Dennett—can be sure that the human genome is not evidence of a creator God.

Our own species is the most prodigious and inscrutable facet of the entire cosmos. Human consciousness and its phenomenal achievements—scientific, philosophic, and cultural—are evidence ("signs, indications") of a cosmic intellect whose creative exploits went beyond matter, with its micro wonders, to create the even more dazzling phenomenon of life; and beyond that, to create consciousness; and beyond that, to create a species of primate with peak specimens like Aristotle, Shakespeare, Newton, Michelangelo, Bach, and Einstein.

Unproven, Not Disproven

"No!" you shout. "That's the old argument from design, resurrected in the lab of particle physics and dressed in the robes of genius. Two hundred years ago, Paley argued that a watch requires a watchmaker. Now Hayes says, 'A genius is a work of genius.' We've put all that behind us." No, we haven't. At most, we've conceded that it's not proof. It doesn't compel belief. But we can't deny it the status of *evidence*. Evidence of a highly probative kind.

The evidence is ambiguous. It may be variously interpreted. But it is evidence of *something exceedingly hard to comprehend. Something vast and mysterious.* Is it a cryptic force of nature, mindless and impersonal? Or a cosmic consciousness that stands apart from the awesome world it produced? A reasonable case can be made for either position.

But we who choose God can legitimately cite the universe—at the macro and micro levels—as evidence for our hypothesis.

chapter 10

Why People
Become Atheists

Would atheists regard it as heresy if I were to allege that most of them, like Christians and other theists, occasionally have doubts? The atheistic doubt, of course, is a suspicion that despite all their well-crafted arguments—and the science that undergirds them—*God may exist*. Some deny that such puerile thoughts ever cross their mind, but others admit they do. The doubting Thomas is not just a Christian phenomenon; skeptics waver, too.

In fact, the same wide range of gradations—from unshakable faith, to strong faith, to fragile faith, to wobbly faith—marks both the atheist and the theist communities. At different times in our lives, we may find ourselves at different places on that spectrum. The unshakable may be shaken; the wobbly may become strong. And every year, each camp boasts converts from the other.

Simplicity vs. Complexity

Since I was once a convert *to* atheism, and later in my life a convert *from* atheism, I know something about conversion and the complex of factors, intellectual and emotional, that bring it about. One advantage atheism has in making converts is that it asks them to assent to an extremely *simple* proposition: there is no God. The Catholic, the Protestant, and the Jew, by contrast, must convince the prospective convert not only that God exists, but that a hundred—nay, a thousand—things about him and his interactions with mankind are true.

The Protestant Bible contains sixty-six books (thirty-nine Old Testament; twenty-seven New Testament); the Catholic Bible contains seventy-three. The prevailing Christian view is that all those books are not only sacred but trustworthy—error free—in every line. Add to this the numerous theological "confessions," one for every Protestant sect, the seven-hundred-page Catechism of the Catholic Church, and Torah and the Talmud for Orthodox Judaism. You can see why *exiting* a formal religion is a streamlined process compared to *entering* one. "It's all rubbish" is a much easier sell than "it's all true, you must believe it, and you must live by it."

Biblical Cruelty Provokes Atheism

For many the complexity of an established religion is not the major problem. They point to one or two dogmas, behavioral rules, or Biblical events, and those are enough to make them recoil from the sect. I am astonished at how often people give scriptural reasons for their atheism. The Christian doctrine of eternal damnation to a fiery hell for grave sin (or because of predestination) terrified many when they were believers. Better to abolish God entirely than live in fear of being immolated by his wrath. Atheism offers escape from that horrific aspect of the Christian worldview. Better no God, some decide, than one who might torment me for eternity.

Some see the God of the Old Testament as unpardonably cruel and obsessed with being worshipped. What kind of God, they say, would demand that Abraham be willing to slaughter his own son with a knife to prove his devotion? But he didn't really demand that, I point out; he relented at the end. He demanded that Abraham be *willing*, they insist, and that was monstrously egocentric.

Slaughter at Jericho

Others point to atrocities that the God of Abraham ordered and did not relent from. When he gave his chosen people the Promised Land, it was filled not only with milk and honey but also with inhabited towns and cities. The residents were living normal lives: working for a living, raising and loving their families. We are not told they were wicked like Sodom and Gomorrah. Yet when Joshua had his army march around the walled city of Jericho, just before the walls collapsed, he said to his people: "Shout; for the LORD has given you the city. And the city and all that is within it shall be devoted to the LORD for destruction . . ." (Josh. 6:16–17).

The trumpet sounded, the people shouted, the wall fell:

> Then they utterly destroyed all in the city, both men and women, young and old, oxen, sheep, and asses, with the edge of the sword. . . . And they burned the city with fire, and all within it; only the silver and gold, and the vessels of bronze and of iron, they put into the treasury of the house of the LORD. (Josh. 6:21, 24)

New Testament Harshness

Atheists can go on, citing dozens of atrocities like these in the Old Testament. Some rival fundamentalists in their knowledge and memory of selected Scriptures. They speak as if such passages were the rule and not the rare exception. To them the Psalms, the Proverbs, the Song of Songs, the illuminations of Isaiah, the wisdom of Ecclesiastes, and the thousand accounts of God's providence are utterly negated by instances of iron-fisted severity.

Many are repelled by the whole Bible, New Testament and Old. But where, you ask, did God do something brutally cruel in the New Testament? I know a Catholic woman who never left the faith but could not forgive God for requiring that his Son be crucified, though Jesus implored, "Let this cup [of torment] pass from me." How could a caring Father turn a deaf ear to that plea? He must have loved his Son much less than she loved hers. My pointing out that Father and Son were one, that God himself paid the price he demanded, and that the sacrificial death redeemed us all, did not avail. She would never have consigned *her* son to the cross. (Since *I* was that son, I smiled indulgently at the heresy.)

Tedious Demands and Impossible Standards

Yet barbaric cruelty, ordered or sanctioned by the deity, is not always the main indictment. For many, the numerous demands and constraints of religious teaching are enough to make God unpalatable. What a killjoy, they protest. He takes all the fun out of life. Who needs him? Who needs this nonsense about dietary laws and keeping holy the Sabbath—dragging yourself out of bed every Sunday morning, even if Saturday's fun kept you up till three?

Sitting through services so boring you couldn't stay awake even if you weren't sleep deprived?

Who can live by the impossible standards Christ preached? All this stuff about loving vicious enemies; turning the other cheek when someone hurts you, blessing those who curse you, lending with no expectation of repayment, going the extra mile for people who oppress you, forgiving a nasty relative 490 times ("seventy times seven"), feeling guilty of adultery if you cast a lustful glance at a woman and defiled if you bed one out of wedlock.

Then the Catholic Church adds that you're in mortal sin if you use a condom *with your wife*. It's all so unnatural and extreme, many say, I'd be a neurotic if I tried to practice it. And I'd be psychotic if I feared that a sin or two would cast me into "outer darkness" where there's "weeping and gnashing of teeth." Talk about fire and brimstone—it's not for me. I not only *don't* believe, I don't *want* to believe!

An Alternative to Organized Religion?

These objections to religion are heartfelt. We can't dismiss them lightly. Even weightier arguments can be made. And there are strong counterarguments to vindicate belief. I will not give them here. Instead, I'll propose an alternative to all organized religion—yet one that organized religion should not object to. But if atheists don't want to hear it, why bother? Read on.

chapter 11

The Only Way Out of Atheism: Pure Theism

However heartfelt the aversion to religion is in many atheists, contrary sentiments sometimes surface. The occasional doubt (a fear that God *may* exist) is not the only chink in their armor. Still more embarrassing, many feel a recurring wish that he *did* exist, because, well . . . he wasn't *all* bad. Atheism delivers us from restraints, inhibitions, and irritations. It does not deliver us from the frailties and vulnerabilities of the human condition. We are weak and mortal in a brutal universe. Whether there is a God or not, *we need one.* Without him, we'll perish—and most of us don't want to.

The Downside of Atheism: Renouncing Hope

Moreover, we have a subliminal hunger that is felt, if seldom recognized—a craving for something ineffably beautiful and good that we can seize and hold and never lose. We want to be happier than anything or anyone has ever made us. The *dream,* in all its splendor, never comes true. Or at least never *stays* true. We must soon learn to love the dream without the splendor. Honeymoon becomes marriage. We must lower expectations and be content with the irksome and mundane, with small love moments, not the enveloping rapture we once tasted, or divorce will follow.

Art, romance, success, wealth, erotic adventure, fame for a few—all can be thrilling, but the thrill fades, the glories fade, *we* fade, and all will be taken from us, or we from it. The only possible satisfaction of our need for *unfading* love, bliss, and glory is God. So, for every atheist who occasionally doubts the infallibility of his denials, and feels the tug of the transcendent, I propose . . . Pure Theism.

One Step out of Atheism

Look anew at the question of God's existence completely apart from the Bible, Judeo-Christian theology, and the theology of any organized religion. The doctrines and Scriptures of Jews, Christians, and Muslims need have no bearing on the elemental question of whether a personal and loving God exists. If he does, we can conceive of him apart from all established theologies and Scriptures. We can commune and build a relationship with him *directly*—without intervention of a rabbi, priest, minister, or imam.

Though I have embraced an organized religion, I was a pure theist for years. For me, it was *the only way out of atheism*. I began with the most simplified and essential concept of a supernatural being: one who created the universe, loves what he made, and follows with benevolent concern the fate of every human life. Not the God of Abraham, not the trinitarian God we Christians believe in, not Jesus, the incarnate Son of God. That would have been too much for me—and I had said no to it again and again. Just *God*, a supreme being who cares about his human creatures and wants a relationship with them. The distance between *no* God and *just* God, Pure Theism, is immeasurable. I was there for two years after atheism, before Christianity became possible for me.

Grasp the Essence

Pure Theism is a life-altering option that should be considered by anyone who cannot accept the images and stories of God—or onerous rules of conduct—that are embedded in established religions. I could not have emerged from atheism directly into any formal religion, so I don't advocate that. Nor do I insist on Christianity (which I've embraced) as the destination for everyone who comes out of atheism. Organized religion is an option but not a requirement for a new believer.

Pure Theism can be the start of a journey, as it was for me—or a harbor where you cast anchor and build a home. Whether you move on or stay, you will not be cosmically alone, as you were before. When the divine penetrates the human, present and future are transformed. You see the world, yourself, and your destiny with a changed eye. You are freed from atheism's demand that you suppress hope in its most luminous forms. Death, though still grim, is transitional. Life, though still hard, has a transcendent source of wisdom and strength—and *a shining Sequel.*

chapter 12

Empirical Theism: A Thought Experiment

What I propose is not a new theology. It is a sliver of existing theologies that one never sees separated from them and standing alone. Pure Theism is that sliver, in its limpid crystalline essence.

The door from atheism to theism opened for me when I read this stunning affirmation by William James: *"We and God have business with each other, and in opening ourselves to His influence our deepest destiny is fulfilled."*

"We and God"—The plain-stated linkage is intriguing. "Have business with each other"—Unpiousness, urbanity, practicality; a suggestion of profitable commerce; an interchange that does not require me to abase myself before starting. Nothing clerical or preachy in this appeal. "And in opening ourselves to His influence"—How easy to visualize! Just stop shutting him out; *open* myself. Well, there's no doubt I've been closed to him. *Influence* has a less intimidating sound than compulsion or command, and is more comprehensible than grace. "Our deepest destiny is fulfilled."—That is what atheism utterly lacks: a stirring destiny. Our future is so short and opaque. However much speed we gather in life, it ends with a crash into the wall of death. They cart our wreckage away, and it's over.

Where New Faith Begins

The powerful sentence by William James, not a verse of Scripture, was the embryo of my Pure Theism. I read 507 pages into *The Varieties of Religious Experience* before I came to it. That book, so charged with the vision, insight, and erudition of a great scientific and philosophical mind, convinced me that believing in God is *intellectually respectable*. The sentence lodged in my brain like a mustard seed and, after much repetition, finally took root.

Call it the James Affirmation. Memorize it. Carry it with you. Gaze at the world for minutes every day through that illuminating lens. Experiment with its insight. Sit still and quiet. Let your breathing become deep and regular. Shut out the myriad distractions and concerns. Suspend your skepticism—relax your white-knuckled grip on it. Repeat the affirmation silently or aloud. Meditate on each of its four elements, one by one:

"We and God."

Those three words brim with the essence of theistic faith. Creature and Creator in a state of mutual awareness. Mutual acknowledgement. Ahh, you say, but I acknowledge only a remote possibility. That's enough, I reply. That's enough for now.

"Have business with each other."

Think of it. A transaction between God and man. Between God and you. You can do something for him, and he can do something for you. Not just *one* transaction, though it begins with that. A working relationship will develop if you let it. A daily interchange. But if there is a God, you ask, what can I do for him? He's infinite, he needs nothing. You can *believe in him*, I reply. Does he need that? No. But *you* need it, so he wants it for you, because you're incomplete without it. He wants you to be complete. Without him, you can't be. And you can't have him if you deny he exists.

"And in opening ourselves to His influence."

How would I open myself, even if I wanted to? you ask. Einstein arrived at his greatest scientific insights not by lab experiments but by what he called "thought experiments." He would imagine what might happen if a certain set of facts came together in a certain way. Often the facts were quite abstract and impossible to duplicate in the material world—for example, a bucket of water rotating in outer space. How would its contents react, given certain gravitational or non-gravitational hypotheses?

Let's emulate the great scientist and do a thought experiment. For the sake of it, and for the moment, imagine that a cosmic intelligence exists. Savor the idea that the supreme benevolent reality is conscious of you, has not rejected you (though you've rejected him), and is eager to connect. He might be there, and he might care, is your first hypothesis. Wade into the depths of that glistening possibility. Yield yourself to its enveloping warmth. Experience its buoyancy.

He might be there, and he might care . . . about *you*, deeply. If that were true, nothing would be the same. Everything would be new. Meditate on the majesty of that thought, and expose your consciousness to its meaning and consequence. Allow yourself to be touched and stirred by the invisible hand that called you out of nothingness—and wants you never to fall into nothingness again. Be passive, receptive, welcoming. Open.

"Our deepest destiny is fulfilled."

What do you think of as *your destiny*? Love. Gratifying friendship. Success in your work, profession, or art. Recognition. Fame. Affluence, even wealth. A splendid place to live. Handsome progeny who achieve distinction. Then a long, serene, travel-filled, and fascinating retirement. Finally, a stately, well-attended memorial service, with eloquent eulogies by the tearful many who loved you and lament your passing. Then a grave, a vault in a mausoleum, or a scattering of your dust on some picturesque land or seascape. An honorable destiny, to be sure. It may satisfy your imagination. *It does not satisfy God's.*

Immortal, he designed you to share his immortality. Timeless, he will bring you beyond time and death to a realm where nothing decays, nothing tarnishes, nothing dies. Great-hearted, he will expand your heart, and help you love people, his world, yourself, and him in a way that will make you stronger and more joyful than you've ever been. He will not deliver you from life's toils, ills, frustrations, losses, and tragedies. But he will help you bear them, get through them, look past them.

Indestructible

You will see things differently when you feel that he, a Spirit, has made *you* part spirit, and that the spirit part of you is indestructible. The bond of love that grows between you and him will be indestructible, too. Breath will cease, but love will endure. And in the silent promise of that love is hid *your deepest destiny*. He will start leading you to its fulfillment—a slow illuminating process—as soon as you ask him to, as soon as you let him. Open yourself. At least a little. Now.

*A Note on Chapter 12:

When I posted a draft of this chapter on my blog, a reader was put off by my talk of love, and in a comment called it "mawkish." I replied:

Poor Words, Rich Truth

I feared that reaction and tried to avoid it, but I can't write about the God of Pure Theism without talking about love, since that's what he is—and what his universe is about. It's a decidedly *tough* love—thorny, punishing, sometimes brutal—but ultimately healing, redemptive, beatific.

Love, as I use the term, is not a feeling. It is *a moral disposition* to show kindness, rather than indifference or malice, to other human beings. The Good Samaritan may have had no feeling of affection for the stricken stranger he helped. His love was in an attitude of empathetic concern and the helping act it generated.

Even in a bad mood, when all feelings are negative, a caring disposition restrains the hurtful impulse and behaves altruistically. Love, in this moral context, is a way of thinking and acting that does not depend on warm emotions. Love of God too is an attitude—of faith, trust, and reverence—that endures through all vicissitudes of circumstance and feeling.

We must be open not only to God but to *his love flowing through us*—to the people in our lives and to others we can only remotely touch. It may sound mawkish when I write about it, but that's a deficit in my writing skill, which I acknowledge. The reality I point to is robust, powerful, and fresh as sunrise.

Shane

chapter 13

Can an Atheist "Choose" to Believe in God?

When I posted on my blog a draft of the last chapter, "Empirical Theism: A Thought Experiment," my feisty reader C. S. said:

> Hmmmm. Can one actually "choose" to believe in God? Speaking for myself, I would find it quite difficult to wake up tomorrow, sit up on the bed, and think to myself, "I guess I'll try believing in God today and see how it works out." What do you think, Shane? To what extent can a person "choose" to believe in God?

My reply

Missionary efforts for the last two thousand years have all been based on the proposition that *a person can choose to believe in God*. Their notable success indicates that the proposition is true. There were a handful of Christians when

Jesus died. Three thousand were converted on Pentecost. Many times that number have been converted to atheism by the books and lectures of Dawkins, Harris, Hitchens, Dennett, and Stenger. The New Atheists wouldn't argue so vigorously if people could not change their minds on the question of God's existence. And I wouldn't be writing this if I didn't think so.

A Key to Inward Change

Perhaps the real thrust of your question is: Can a sophisticated, widely-read atheist in this era *choose* to believe in God? My answer is an emphatic yes—but with a qualifier appended: if he wants to. In Chapter Five, I made a statement that I'll quote here in a context that gives it different emphasis:

Among several important things I can't prove but am convinced of is this: in deciding whether or not to believe in God, no one, on either side of the issue, is completely objective. Nor *should* one be, since the arguments are weighty on both sides, and neither side proves its case. Evidence and logic leave us dangling. In forming an opinion of what is unknowable, personal considerations become relevant, even determinative.

The Role of Desire in Belief

On the question of God's existence, most people end up believing what they want to believe. There is much weighing of evidence and pondering of argument, but these don't produce a conclusive yes or no. So a subtle—often complex—form of *personal preference* carries the day. I am a Christian because I *want* to be, and you are an atheist because you *want* to be. Until the wanting changes, neither of us is likely to budge. But if the wanting did change, we could change, too.

I don't mean we can push a mental button and transmute in an instant. It might take months or years of intense grappling with evidence, argument, and our inner lives. But evidence and argument depend so much on the light in which we view them, and that light is so determined by our psyches (which is what I mean by *our inner lives*), that an atheist can, ultimately, choose to believe in God if he wants to.

A theist, too, can go the other way. Every year, a great many convert to the opposite view. The New Atheists pull them toward No God. I in my way—and organized religions in theirs—try to pull them toward God. Self-determination in such matters is the rule, not the exception.

Three Factors That Make Choosing Possible

To illustrate the difficulty of the change, its possibility, and an essential element in it, let me cite a human-interest tale from the New Testament. A father pleading with Jesus to heal his ailing son said, "if *you can do anything*, have pity on us and help us." Jesus echoed his doubting phrase: "'*If* you can! All things are possible to him who believes.' Immediately the father of the child cried out and said, 'I believe; help my unbelief!'" (Mark 9:22–24, emphasis added.) Jesus healed the child.

The skeptic, of course, will dismiss this as myth. My purpose here is not to argue for its truth but to make a psychological point.

The episode highlights three principles:

1. The starting point is *a desire to believe*—the father *wanted* to think help was there;
2. Belief can be mingled with unbelief;
3. *Conscious effort* may be needed to acquire faith and banish doubt.

I present the incident not as an argument for Christianity, but to show the elements of transition from atheism to pure theism. The man in the story needed help. An atheist who contemplates a change of mind (and heart) may—or may not—do so because he feels a need for strength beyond what human resources provide. Someone said, "Man's extremity is God's opportunity." I have found that to be so. Those who feel weak are probably more open to faith than those who feel strong. But this doesn't mean the strong are right and the weak are wrong.

The Bold Crossing

A skeptic who acknowledges there *may* be a God, and would like to connect with him if it's possible, must take a bold step. He must move from abstract thought to a new kind of consciousness that is both outreaching and receptive. In Chapter Twelve, "Empirical Theism: A Thought Experiment," I describe a bridge from the mental to the spiritual, and try to walk the reader across it, as I crossed it decades ago. That movement shows how an atheist who wants to can begin moving toward belief in God and a relationship with him. Yes, my atheist friend, you can *choose* to believe. There's a way out of atheism.

Part 2

Boy in a Storm
(A Portrait of the Author at Seventeen in a Faith Crisis–Autobiographical Fiction)

Boy in a Storm

I am not a religious man. Yet I am a staunch Catholic. Staunch rather than devout. That's because it's my nature to be staunch but not my nature to be devout. And one must accept one's nature. Not everyone concedes this. You have on the one hand Catholics who accept their natures and on the other Catholics who don't. The distinction is not simple.

Before I become too metaphysical, let me step back in time, over half a century, and introduce Larry O'Toole, since this is his story. A high school senior, age seventeen, he had convinced himself that he wanted to become a Trappist monk. Yes, a Trappist— the ones who commit to perpetual silence, live in extreme poverty, do hard manual labor, and vow never to leave the monastery. One afternoon, he was sitting at the kitchen table, arguing with his mother. Her cheeks were flushed with vexation. Her brilliant son was making another incontrovertible point.

"It's a matter of simple logic," he was saying. (He was always being logical. That was his most unpleasant trait.) "'God made us to know him, to love him, and to serve him in this world, and to be happy with him forever in heaven.' That's my whole case in a nutshell. It's from the *Baltimore Catechism*, and you gave it to me when I was six."

"I did not," she protested.

"Well, you sent me to the nuns, and the nuns gave it to me. The Christian Brothers and priests have confirmed it all through high school. It's quite simple: the world is a place of suffering, trial, and purification. Happiness isn't meant to be our lot here. It's a reward for earthly suffering. We should struggle through our time here as best we can. If a bit of happiness falls our way, it's a preview. An earnest of things to come. Not a lasting part of our natural state."

"Your eloquence is boring," she said. "You talk like a book."

"I *am* a book," he replied, "and I plan to have a happy ending. But it's a long way off, and I have a lot of pages to turn before I get there. Look, happiness is the thing we want most. I concede that. But *there*, not here, is the place to find it."

"Where?" his father interposed, having quietly entered the room. Larry looked up at Matt O'Toole and nodded a greeting.

"In heaven, where God is."

"God is everywhere," Matt observed.

Larry ignored him. "The question is how to get *there* as safely and directly as possible. God made me, and I'm living for him. Well, then, let me *live* for him. If he's the prime purpose of my existence, then let me live each day as if this were the only fact."

"There are *lots* of other facts," his mother pointed out.

"Yes, but they're minor and they all add up to this one: we should live for God. How shall I do this, and where shall I go?" He held up his hand. "Please don't interrupt. That was a rhetorical question. The best thing is to look around, find someone who's doing it well and follow him. Looking around, I see that not many are doing it well. Not many seem to be trying. Not many even care. This puzzles me, because the people I have in mind are Catholics, who share my premises. Why don't they reach the obvious conclusion and live for God alone, if he's the chief purpose of their existence? Why doesn't it even occur to them?"

"Because they're not fanatics," Matt replied.

"It's not fanaticism; it's rationality."

"Same thing," his mother said. "Listening to you, it sounds like the same thing."

Matt agreed. "Your whole stand is too extreme," he said.

Larry had an answer ready: "Every conclusion is the extreme end of a syllogism. You shouldn't go around giving kids premises if you don't want them to draw conclusions."

That sounded right. But something was wrong.

Matt tried a different tack. "All your friends went to the same Catholic schools you did. They had the same nuns, Christian Brothers, and priests. They got the same ... premises, as you put it. But they don't have your radical—upside down—view of life. They want to have a good time, go to college. Drink and party a little. Get a good job, make a living. Date, marry, and have kids. Catholic teaching doesn't keep them from doing *any* of that. Why are you and your Catholic friends so different? There are seven hundred fifty guys in your class at West. How many are going to run off to a monastery?"

Larry shrugged. "Just one that I know of."

"Is he the only sane one or the only nut?"

Larry sighed. He thought of some things he wanted to say, but preferred not to say them in front of his mother. He asked if he could talk to his father alone. His mother was offended, at first. Perceiving that, he said, "Mom, we need some *man talk* that wouldn't be quite right in front of a lady." She seemed mollified and left the room, looking more hurt than angry.

When the door was closed, Larry said, "Dad, I don't want to knock my friends. I know I'm an oddball in the way I think. They're good guys. God bless 'em, I love 'em. But they don't follow religious premises to their logical conclusions. Religion is a little compartment in their mind. Like a drawer. They put all the religious stuff in there. It means something to them. They value it, in a way. But then they close the drawer and don't open it 'til Saturday afternoon, when they have to tell their sins in confession. And when they leave Mass on Sunday, they close the drawer for another week and don't think about it.

"I can't do that. I carry it with me . . . everywhere. I believe in God, and heaven, and hell. That's what life is really about. It's about whether we get to heaven or we don't. Our religion course, every year, teaches about mortal sin. A mortal sin puts you in hell for eternity if you die with it on your soul. Dad, I commit a lot of mortal sins. From impure thoughts to . . . talks on the corner about sex . . . to stuff I do with girls at drive-ins. Most of my life, I walk around with mortal sins on my soul. Saturday afternoon I go to confession, and I leave in a state of grace. But by nine or ten that night, I'm at a drive-in necking with a girl.

"We don't do much. I'm still a virgin. But if I French kiss her, that's a mortal sin. If I touch her breast, that's a mortal sin. If I just go on hugging and kissing once I get passionate, even if I don't do anything else, that's a mortal sin. This is church teaching, and all the guys hear it. My friend Dan jokes that there's only one way we'll get to heaven. If we walk out of confession at five o'clock on Saturday afternoon, and get hit by a car *before* we get to the drive-in four hours later. If we die during that four-hour period, we go to heaven. The rest of the week, we're cooked." He smiled faintly.

Matt shook his head and chuckled.

"Yeah, we laugh," Larry said. "But what are we laughing at? Is the church teaching a joke? Is it a bunch of crap? Or are we taking it too lightly? If it's true, we're taking it too lightly. If hell is real, it's horrible—fire and agony—and it never ends. Should we spend 98 percent of every week bound for hell? Is that any way to live? Is that a *rational* way to live?"

With a dismissive wave, Matt said, "No one thinks of it that way. A mortal sin is hard to commit."

"Not for me and Nick it's not. Not for our friends and classmates. It's not just church teaching, it's in the Bible. Jesus said if you even look at a woman with lust in your heart, you commit adultery. Dad, we look at girls with lust in our hearts every day. We joke about mortal sin, but we're in it all the time. It's hard for you to commit a mortal sin because you're married. Sex is allowed. Sure, I could have sinless sex if I married. Do you want me to get married?"

"Not at seventeen, with no college and no job."

"When would it make sense for me to marry?"

"When you're out of college and start making a living."

"Dad, that's four years away. Most of that four years, I'd be in mortal sin. Think of the risk—if the church is right, and hell is real. Do you see the logic of my concern? Where's the flaw in my logic?"

"By your logic, every one of those seven hundred fifty guys in your class should run off to a monastery to hide from temptation. Does *that* make sense? Does the church say they should? The monasteries couldn't hold them!"

Larry looked perplexed. "Dad, I don't know what makes sense for them. They have to figure out their own lives. I only know what makes sense for me. I don't even know *that*, but I'm trying hard to think clearly and reach logical conclusions. Maybe my logic only works for people who have a vocation. I think I have one. I'm not sure, but I think so.

"And fear of hell isn't the only thing. I love God, too. I don't just fear him. I love God. I love Christ. Nothing matters more than being close to God. Nothing would be worse than losing him. And losing heaven. I want to live a life that puts those values first. Above everything. Thomas Merton has done that. The other Trappist monks have done that. They're leading *great* lives. Saintly lives. The nuns and priests are leading good lives too. But I want to live a *great* spiritual life, like Merton. I want to be a Trappist."

The upshot of all this verbalizing was Matt's agreement to help Larry visit a Trappist monastery so he could talk to them about entering. Matt said he'd make a call the next day.

That night, around midnight, he burst into Larry's room and startled him.

"Why are you kneeling there pounding your chest?" he demanded.

Larry looked up at him in great annoyance. Matt was afraid Larry would say something rude. But he restrained himself.

"Because I read in a book that you should kneel down and pound your chest, that's why I'm doing it. Don't you knock before entering?"

"Your chest is all red. I could hear you across the hall."

"I know it's red. I'm sorry about the noise."

Larry was kneeling there, waiting for Matt to go.

"Well, why in God's name are you doing it?" Matt asked, exasperated.

Larry raised his eyes to the ceiling and summoned all his patience. Forcing a caustic smile, he said, "So I'll get a higher place in heaven. Now will you leave me alone?"

Larry's parents, Matt and Mae O'Toole, were practicing Catholics whose faith was important to them. They believed, prayed at home and in church, never missed Mass and Communion on Sunday, and contributed generously to the church. Missals, prayer books, rosaries, miraculous medals, and crucifixes were valued possessions, visible around the house. They sent Larry to Catholic grade school and high school, and hoped he would attend a Catholic college. The parish priests, and the nuns who taught all eight grades of elementary school, were revered figures in his life.

There was a native piety in Larry. He responded more than most children to religious teaching at home and in school. From early childhood, he felt awe at the idea of God, his presence everywhere (*every*where!), and his embodiment in the man Jesus. Parents and nuns conveyed to him, very successfully, a sense of the beautiful and the sacred. The two were so allied—so derived from the same essence—that he saw beauty in things religious and felt the sacred in natural beauty. The supreme ineffable goodness and purity of Christ came to him *visually* long before he received it narratively or doctrinally. It radiated from paintings, holy picture cards, statuary, and crucifixes. The crucifix came in many sizes: tiny ones, half the size of your thumb, on rosaries and on gold chains around women's necks; hand-size ones on the habits of nuns; arm-size ones centered high on the front wall of every classroom; and life-size ones above the altars in some churches.

Catholics believe in the doctrine of transubstantiation: that at the words of consecration—"This is my body; this is my blood"—the bread and wine are mysteriously and invisibly transformed into the physical presence of Christ. Since consecrated hosts (wafers) were kept in the tabernacle (large gold container) on the altar of every church, the doctrine of the "real presence" holds that Jesus, in that mysterious and invisible way, is physically present in a Catholic church. The vigil light, a candle flickering inside a small lamp with red glass panels, must always be lit—even in a locked and empty church—to acknowledge the sacred presence.

For Larry, entering a church and praying there was like entering the Holy of Holies in the Old Testament: he was with God, and God in Christ was there as truly and palpably as if he were a few feet away, hidden in the shadows. The maker of the universe had become incarnate in Christ; Christ had said to his followers "I am with you always"; and in sacramental form, he was more "with you" when you knelt before the altar of his church than anywhere else. As Larry learned to love God, and his crucified risen Son, he learned also to love the church as an institution founded by Christ, and the church buildings where the divine seemed to touch the earth and embrace the human.

When he was still a very young kid—and not even a very nice kid—his belief in these doctrines became a vivid and moving part of how he saw the world, human history, and his place in the ongoing drama. More and more he did not think of himself or his future apart from God, and he did not think of God apart from the Catholic Church. He wanted to unite as closely as possible with both.

When he was fifteen, his parents read a bestselling book by a Trappist monk named Thomas Merton, *The Seven Storey Mountain*. They spoke of Merton as being a "deep" thinker and said the book was intellectually challenging. His curiosity stirred, Larry sampled the book, found it wasn't beyond him, read it, and was profoundly impressed by Merton's evolution from worldly intellectual to contemplative monk. The term "contemplative monk" is an abstraction that conveys little of the rigor and austerity of Trappist life. The formal name of the monastic group Merton joined is the Order of Cistercians of the Strict Observance. The order took the name "Trappist" from La Trappe Abbey in Normandy, France, where it began as a reform movement in 1664 to tighten the relaxed practices that had crept into many Cistercian monasteries. Cistercian, or Trappist, monks commit themselves to poverty, celibacy, obedience, stability (never to leave the monastery), and a strict rule of silence. These excerpts from the *Catholic Encyclopedia* give some sense of extreme Trappist austerity:

The hour for rising is at 2 a.m. on weekdays, 1:30 on Sundays, and 1 on the more solemn feasts; whilst the hour for retiring is at 7 p.m. in winter, and 8 in summer; . . . so that the religious have seven hours' sleeping in the course of the day; about seven hours also are devoted to the Divine Office and Mass, one hour to meals, four hours to study and private prayers and five hours to manual labour. . . . [Note that there is not an hour, not a minute, set apart for socializing; and meals though taken together must be eaten in silence.]

The monks are obliged to live by the labour of their hands, so the task appointed for manual labour is seriously undertaken, and is of such a nature as to render them self-supporting; such as cultivation of the land, cattle-raising, etc. . . . Food consists of bread, vegetables, and fruits. . . . Flesh-meat, fish, and eggs are forbidden at all times, except to the sick.

All sleep in a common dormitory, the beds being divided from each other only by a partition and curtain, the bed to consist of mattress and pillow stuffed with straw, and sufficient covering. The monks are obliged to sleep in their regular clothing; which consists of ordinary underwear, a habit of white, and a scapular of black wool, with a leathern cincture; the cowl, of the same material as the habit, is worn over all. Enclosure [the requirement to remain in the monastery], according to canon law, is perpetual in all houses.

It is never allowed for the religious to speak amongst themselves, though the one in charge of a work or employment may give necessary directions; and all have the right of conversing with the superiors at any time except during the night hours, called the "great silence."

Naturally, Larry found most of this grim and daunting. But Merton so successfully extolled and embodied the moral elevation, the spiritual richness, of the Trappist life that Larry was drawn to it. If God is "the prime purpose of our existence," and if renouncing the world is the best way to live "for God alone" and enter into profound communion with him, Larry thought he should do it. He less than halfheartedly wanted to.

In fact, he wanted all kinds of things incompatible with monastic life, principal among them being a love relationship with a girl. Merton had wanted that too and had put it behind him. Jesus said, "If any man would come after me, let him deny himself and take up his cross daily and follow me. For whoever would save his life will lose it, and whoever loses his life for my sake will find it" (Matt. 16:24–25). Larry would try to lose his life, as Merton had—and find it in a Trappist monastery, as Merton had.

Matt and Mae O'Toole, religious as they were, thought the Trappist idea bordered on insanity. They wanted Larry to get a job, find a nice girl, marry, and have children—in other words, live a normal life. They were Catholic enough to be glad there were priests and nuns. They appreciated what those dedicated people contributed to the running of parishes, the sacramental and prayer life of the congregation, and the education of children. But they thought mandatory celibacy was abnormal and unhealthy and had wanted no part of it themselves. In their view, becoming a Trappist would be a tragedy for their son. Think of the things he'd never have: a woman in his life, the joy of begetting and raising a family, a home of his own, and a career, in any earthly sense of the term.

He would leave all his friends behind and never see them again. When a Trappist takes his final vows, he promises to live his whole life within the confines of the monastery. Communications with and visits from his family are severely restricted. All those sacrifices, and more, fall under the rubric of "leaving the world." As if that were not stark enough, he wouldn't even have a normal social life *in* the monastery, because the rule of silence barred conversation with his fellow monks most of the time. His parents made all these arguments repeatedly during his last two years of high school. He was not persuaded.

In the forward to his historical work on monasticism *The Waters of Siloe*, Thomas Merton gives a list of the renunciations and austerities that Trappist monks endure. He goes on to say:

> When you ask . . . these men why they have done such things they may give you a very clear answer or, perhaps, only a rather confused answer, but in either case it will amount to this: . . . They have felt the terrible insufficiency of life in a civilization that is entirely dedicated to the pursuit of shadows. What is the use of living for things . . . you cannot hold on to, values that crumble . . . as soon as you possess them, pleasures that turn sour before you have begun to taste them, and a peace that is constantly turning to war? (xviii)

In other words, their decision was formed in the womb of disillusionment and discontent. That one passage of Merton's writing crystallized Larry's jumbled impressions and feelings. He thought it the most illuminating statement he had ever read. And the most vindicating. Never had he viewed *unhappiness* in such a flattering light. It made *his* unhappiness seem enlightened and sanctified— not the result of adolescent deficiencies and maladjustments, but of valid reactions to a tarnished world. It implied that the wisest men raise themselves above the deceptions and corruptions of ordinary life; they ascend heavenward, Godward, by entering monasteries.

Larry broke off with a cute little blond girl halfway through senior year. As graduation neared, his father reluctantly arranged for him to make a five-day retreat at a Trappist monastery. There were closer ones, but Larry insisted on visiting the monastery where Thomas Merton lived: The Abbey of Gethsemani in very rural Trappist, Kentucky. If he was going to enter, why not go where he might catch a glimpse of the living saint whose books had brought him there, the literary giant whose life and writings had awakened the world to an ascetic spirituality that few had been aware of, ancient as it was?

"Gethsemane was the garden where Jesus spent the most agonizing hours of his life, before the crucifixion," Matt pointed out. "His anguish was so intense that he broke out in a bloody sweat." Then he added half facetiously: "Maybe an abbey with a more cheerful name would be a happier place. Is there a Bethlehem Abbey or a Cana Abbey?"

"No, Dad," Larry said. "If you want to avoid Gethsemane, you don't become a Trappist. That was the right one for Merton, and it's the right one for me."

The trip was in late June of 1956, a week after Larry's graduation. His mother and his close friend, Nick Bruni, with whom he had double-dated every weekend until he began practicing for celibacy, saw him off at the airport. His parents and Nick viewed the matter as a tragedy that could still be averted.

They were anxious to give him the feeling that he had committed himself to nothing, that the trip was just an excursion to satisfy his curiosity, and that when he returned, he was expected to forget the whole affair. For all their round display of optimism, they were afraid. He was unpredictable. One never quite knew what was going on inside him. They hoped for the best.

As soon as he had waved good-bye and the plane was in the air, Larry experienced a great sense of isolation. The sky was too vast and vacant, the clouds were too cold and gray, there was no one around him but strangers, and the earth was too far away. He reached into the pocket of his suit coat and felt for his rosary. Keeping his hand in his pocket he leaned back, closed his eyes, and began to pray: "Hail Mary, full of grace, the Lord is with thee. Blessed art thou amongst women, and blessed is the fruit of thy womb, Jesus. Holy Mary. . . ." Hail Mary . . . Holy Mary . . . Lovely Mary.

Mary was the name of the little blond he had broken off with. She wasn't beautiful but decidedly cute . . . and extremely kissable. She had fallen for Larry harder than Larry had fallen for her. But he *did* like her, and breaking off had hurt him, too. A couple of weeks after he had stopped seeing her, she had appeared at the 6:30 morning Mass Larry attended on weekdays. He went every day, but he knew she never did; though Catholic, she was a public school kid and rarely went even on Sundays. She had come only to see him, catch his eye, and revive the romance.

Larry was flattered, attracted, and distracted. Her presence made prayer almost impossible, evoked memories of delicious necking at drive-in movies, and the closeness of four couples—she and Larry one of them—who got together every weekend and made the world feel like a warm and welcoming place. She represented everything he had to leave behind if he was going to follow this higher calling; in a phrase, go Merton's way. Her presence in the church that morning was a test. He had to pass it sooner or later if he was serious about becoming a contemplative priest.

He stayed in the pew a few minutes after Mass was over but couldn't stay long because he had to leave for school. As he left the church, Mary was lingering on the steps about twenty feet away. She smiled and waved at him, obviously hoping he would come and talk with her. His impulse was to take her hands, say, "God, it's good to see you!" and plant a kiss on her wonderfully supple lips. Instead he smiled, nodded politely as if she were a casual acquaintance, walked past her down the steps, and resolutely home, without looking back. He sensed her heartbreak and would remember that incident always as one of the most callous acts of his life. But arriving home he sighed deeply, bit his lip, and reflected that he had passed the test.

His next memory of her was when, about two months later, they sat across from each other at the same table at a nightclub Larry's class went to after the senior prom. Nick had talked Larry out of skipping the prom, since all the guys were going, even those who never dated. It was a hugely important class social event. You had to be part of it, even if you had no interest in the girl you brought.

Mary had been snapped up by one of Larry's classmates as soon as word got out that they had stopped dating. She looked appealing in her pale-blue gauzy prom gown with a neckline that was modest yet showed she had plenty to hide. Larry brought a girl his sister had fixed him up with for the prom. During dinner, he and Mary more than once locked eyes with long silent glances that said, quite mutually, "I wish I were with you. We belong together." She sat with the other guy's arm around her, but her visual message was clear. Larry's was too, and at that moment, he meant it as much as she did.

Mary... Hail Mary.... After blundering through the whole five decades of the rosary, he did not feel sanctified, strengthened, or consoled. In fact, he felt rather worse than before. Taking out *Seeds of Contemplation*, a book by Merton, he began paging through it at random, stopping to read parts of the chapter entitled "Detachment": "Everything you love for its own sake, outside of God alone, blinds your intellect and destroys your judgment of moral values and vitiates your choices so that you cannot clearly distinguish good from evil and you do not truly know God's will..." (124).

Larry was uneasily aware that he had never loved anything, from Mary on down, for any sake other than its own. His affection for Mary was so strong and enveloping that it didn't require supernatural stimulation. It was unsettling to think that this feeling must "blind his intellect and destroy his judgment of moral values," that it must "vitiate his choices" so that he could not "clearly distinguish good from evil" or "truly know God's will." He would have to love her henceforth—*in absentia*, of course—only as a child of God with a spiritual destiny and a soul capable of sanctifying grace.

Larry had to strain to view Mary in that light. No doubt that was because he did not "see things as they really are." His friendship with Nick Bruni was not based on anything religious. It seemed odd to think of linebacker Nick with his barbells and bruising tackles—not to mention his romantic escapades—as "a child of God." But of course he *was* that; even he would admit it if pressed. Larry realized how far he was from holiness, from seeing people in the divine perspective Merton had mastered.

Reading more *Seeds of Contemplation*, he was dismayed that the great man dismissed even feelings of spiritual serenity and consciousness of God's presence as "the miserable little consolations that are given to beginners in the contemplative way.... [N]othing that . . . we can enjoy or desire with our natural faculties can be anything but an obstacle to the pure possession of Him as He is in Himself . . ." (127, 130).

Was it possible, Larry reflected, that God could be content with nothing less than a vacuum in our emotional life? He had not suspected that even the loftiest feelings could be such wayward things. The sentiments that to him had seemed the very essence of religion and sacred beyond all else were now called impediments to spiritual growth. It was bewildering.

Larry remembered that flight to Kentucky vividly all his life. There was a pretty southern girl who got on the plane at Washington, blond, creamy skinned, satin lipped, and lovely, with sea blue eyes and a slumberous drawl. She sat across the aisle from him, chatting amiably with a soldier whom Larry envied passionately. He decided she was one of many things he would be given on the other side of eternity. (He thought heaven would contain—besides the beatific vision of God—fulfillment of deeply felt desires that are frustrated in human life. This was a cherished part of his personal creed; he had no church sanction for it and hoped it wasn't heresy.)

In the train depot in Louisville, he saw a girl who could not have been more than sixteen waiting in the station with a baby in her arms, and he wondered if her husband knew she was a large part of paradise. Larry boarded a train for Bardstown, the station nearest to the abbey. Looking out the windows, he was appalled at the impoverished shanties along the tracks, where poor half-clothed whites lived out their squalid lives. At least they were allowed to speak, he reflected. The men had their women, the women had their men, and both had their children. He could imagine a sorrier life.

Disembarking from the train in the darkness, he found that another passenger was bound for the monastery. A thin soft-spoken man of about thirty-five, he was unprepossessing but friendly and likeable. They asked around and learned that the abbey was two miles up the road and that no cab service or public transportation was available. So they picked up their luggage and trudged through the darkness. A two-mile walk with heavy suitcases was a challenge when they were already fatigued from a long trip and ready to fall into bed.

There were no street lights and even houses were rare along the way, so for long distances, the only light was from the sky. Though it was moonless, the stars were brilliant, and there seemed to be ten times as many as Larry had ever seen before. The air seemed luminous. Larry's companion was a businessman from Cincinnati, who seemed shocked when Larry asked him if he intended to join the order. He said nothing could be further from his mind. He made retreats at monasteries every summer, and very few of the people he met there had any thought of staying permanently.

After walking for what seemed an endless time, they heard children playing on a nearby farm. They found them, asked directions, and were told courteously but ungrammatically that the monks' place wasn't no more than a mile down that there road. A mile! This was only the halfway point. They stretched their aching fingers to get the blood circulating, picked up their bags (which now seemed filled with lead), and pressed on.

After what felt like the longest mile of their lives, they came to a gravel driveway the length of a football field. It was lined with trees and defined by whitewashed rocks at ten-foot intervals. At the end of it, they could discern a high gate, dimly lit, below the outline of a cross. They found the gate locked. It was nine thirty, and silence reigned. The inscription on the archway, "Pax Intrantibus" (Peace on Those Who Enter), had been taken seriously by the inmates: the abbey was asleep. After a long journey and an arduous walk, the thought of spending the night on the ground outside the walls was disheartening. Searching for another means of ingress, Larry decided he would climb over the gate before he'd resign himself to sleeping on the steps. Would he be the first man to sneak *into* a Trappist monastery? He suspected that over the centuries, a few had snuck out.

Finally his companion noticed a kind of cowbell hung beside the entrance. He pulled a rope and rang it. In the nocturnal hush, its loud metallic clang made them feel like children who had yelled in church. Moments later, a monk opened the gate and ushered them in. He was an old man, heavyset, morose, rough-featured, and bald except for the tonsure, an inch-wide rim of hair that encircles a monk's head like a halo. His manner was perfunctory but not rude; they had no doubt woken him from a sound sleep. He wore a burlap cassock that came down to his knees. His calves were wrapped in rags that looked like pieces of an old sheet not remarkable for their cleanliness. On his feet, he wore heavy beat-up workman's boots that looked like they had been fished out of a trash can. He made no effort at small talk. Larry supposed the rule of silence either precluded that or made it hard for want of practice. Taking them to the guesthouse, he had them sign their names in a large book.

He showed them to their rooms, which were hardly more than cells. Though clean and well kept, there was space for only a cot and a small writing board that folded down from the wall. The dimensions were no more than five feet by nine feet. There was only one window and no cross ventilation. Outside it was hot and humid, not the hint of a breeze, and the cell was insufferably close. As fatigued as he was, Larry lay miserably awake all night. He tossed and squirmed on his hard cot as little as possible because it was so narrow and movement made him perspire. Even lying still, he was covered with a sticky film of sweat.

In the shadows, he could discern the outline of a crucifix and a few holy pictures of the Virgin and St. Joseph that were tacked to the wall, the only decoration. He looked at them and tried to pray. He thanked God for the misery and loneliness he was experiencing, because it was a privilege to participate in the sufferings of Christ and because it would earn him, as they said, "a higher place in heaven." Taught that the monstrous sinfulness of the world required endless expiation, and that the greater the suffering the greater the reward, he got out of bed and knelt on the hardwood floor, saying the rosary. He prayed and prayed until his knees ached and his back ached, and when his head swooned with drowsiness, he shook it off and prayed some more.

This was his new life, the life of sacrifice, contrition, expiation, and mortification. Nuns, priests, and contemplative literature said that such things were pleasing to God, helped to release souls from the flaming torments of purgatory, and sanctified one's own soul. The more refined and excruciating the self-inflicted anguish, the more it pleased God. He had read of saints who ate the flies that stuck to their food because God had put them there and to remove them would violate his holy will. Francis of Assisi kissed the rotting lips of lepers whose suffering he tried to alleviate. One saint allowed his body to be infested by flesh-eating insects. Many wore shirts of rough horsehair against their skin so they would always have suffering to offer to God. Others scourged themselves across the back with a cat o' nine tails until they bled and fainted with pain. Not only did the Lord chastise his own, ascetics thought he liked his own to chastise themselves.

Larry remembered sins he had committed. The sin of impurity was his besetting weakness, as it was for Nick and the other guys they ran with. Not that they *did* very much, but sexual thoughts were often on their minds, and erotic designs in their hearts. Never mind that female hands slapped them or pushed them away. Sin is in the will, and they were guilty of what they tried to do, or even planned to attempt. The thought of an erotic act, deliberately savored, was a mortal sin, which would damn you to hell if you died before confessing it. Nuns had said each sin we commit is like driving a nail into the hand of Christ, so intensely did he suffer.

Considering this, Larry beat himself violently on his bare chest with a clenched fist, beat himself again and again until he feared the bones would break and the hollow thuds awaken the other guests. Finally he collapsed on the floor, weeping quietly to himself, convulsed in a knot of misery. More than anything else in the world, he wanted to die. If only he were old and knew that God would take him soon. That was the great thing, to be taken, to know that the protracted nausea of life was near its end, and that soon he would vomit out his soul and be done with it. But he was so young; it could be fifty years before that great release would come. Half a century of this and worse. How many days, how many nights? That was the blackest part, the waiting. Waiting is the quintessence of hell, more agonizing than fire. If he could fit it all into a week or a month or even a year, no matter how bad the pain was, he could stand it. But fifty years!

Though he had nearly despaired of it, morning came at last. At five o'clock, one of the monks walked through the hall of the guesthouse ringing a bell. He announced that Mass would be said in the rear balcony of the main church at five thirty. The church was designed in the Gothic style. Its vertically beamed walls swept upward and inward, converging at their crest to form a long tunnel of high pointed arches, which led the eye forward to a brilliant stained-glass window, then downward to a wide marble altar under a gold tabernacle. In its blending of light and shadow and the austere simplicity of its lines, it was as imposing as any cathedral.

There were only six guests that morning, and the Mass on the church's rear balcony was an intimate affair. The improvised altar was the size of a dressing table and wholly without ornament. The ceremony was sober, devout, and impressive. There was no sermon, and it was over in less than twenty minutes. After Mass, there was a half hour of reflection, followed by the first conference of the day.

Guests were gathered into a small room where the monk who had been appointed retreat master for the year seated himself at a desk and discoursed to them on some pious subject. The conferences lasted about three quarters of an hour.

The retreat master was a small Englishman of middle age, fair skinned, womanish, and prissy. Larry thought he had the softest, whitest hands he had ever seen on a man. How could those hands have done the manual labor required by Cistercian rule? He seemed more like a nun than a priest, though kindhearted and innocuous. Larry had expected something more rugged, sharp-featured, and intense in a Trappist monk: a compound of the intelligence of Merton, the impressiveness of a bishop, and the sturdiness of a peasant.

The sermon was more disappointing than the man himself. Did he think he was addressing twelve-year-olds? At one point, touching on chastity, he expressed the curious view that one should avoid nakedness even in one's own presence. This suggested practical difficulties, but no one questioned it.

The guests were told to be silent during breakfast. Sermons by Fulton Sheen were played over a loudspeaker. The food was good. After breakfast, guests were given a free period. They could sit on the terrace and read spiritual books and periodicals that were distributed for their perusal. If they preferred, they could fraternize or sit in silence and watch a lone monk driving a tractor in a field of wheat, a peaceful scene. Then there was another conference, followed by solemn high Mass at nine o'clock in the main church, which was attended by the entire community, both priest and lay brother. The Abbot said the Mass, assisted by various monastic dignitaries.

The monks wore hooded robes called cowls. As each entered the church, instead of genuflecting before the altar, he would bow deeply from the waist, don his hood, and take his place in the seats or "stalls." These were arranged parallel to the walls of the church and perpendicular to the altar, so that one half of the congregation faced the other half, the altar being to the right or left of each group. When the service began and a signal was given, they raised their voices in the haunting melodious harmonies of Gregorian chant.

The rest of the day was filled with conferences, lunch, more conferences, the stations of the cross, a free hour, dinner, then gathering once more in the church for vespers and benediction. Three days went by rather mechanically in this fashion, and three nights which for Larry were deplorably like the first, though less convulsive. On the morning of the fourth day, each guest was given a private interview with the retreat master. In the course of Larry's, he said he was thinking seriously about joining the order.

The monk seemed pleased. "How long have you been thinking about it?" he asked.

"Over two years."

The priest nodded approvingly. That three-word answer allayed all doubt. "It's a hard life," he said, "and not always a happy one. By no means always a happy one. But if you're going to enter, you should do it with a whole heart. Make it known to everyone at home—family and friends—that you're taking a permanent step, and there will be no turning back. Give away your clothes, your money, everything you own. Don't look over your shoulder. Burn your bridges behind you."

Larry was stunned by the swiftness of the man's transition from viewing him as a casual visitor on retreat to one making an unshakeable commitment to monastic life. Larry had expected at least a trace of his parents' concern that it might be the wrong step for him. Instead, the priest leaped to the conviction that the boy's decision was a fait accompli.

"When you enter the monastery, you should realize that you're *discarding your personal identity.* You'll no longer be . . ."—he looked at a notepad in front of him—"Larry O'Toole. You'll take a new name; the name of a saint. They'll shave off your hair except for the thin tonsure. You'll wear a rough burlap cassock like the rest of us. There will be no social conversation. You'll live by a strict rule of silence. You can speak only to your superiors and your confessor. Only in special cases to guests of the monastery. For all other purposes, you'll be taught the sign language."

Larry nodded with grave assent, visualizing each new reality.

"You'll do at least five hours of manual labor each day. Some in the fields. Some inside. You'll be responsible for whatever job you're given, whether it's washing dirty underwear, peeling potatoes, scrubbing a toilet, or carrying garbage. You take a vow of obedience, so you do whatever your superiors tell you. You don't pick and choose, you don't argue, you don't complain. The duties you're given will be yours for an indefinite time—months, years, your whole life, if they so direct."

He paused to consider what other austerities and trials he should warn of. Larry sensed that to some extent he was warning and to some extent boasting of what he himself had learned to bear.

"You'll take a vow of stability, which means you won't be allowed to leave the monastery for another abbey unless you're transferred by the order. A monk is not even allowed to go home in the event of a parent's death or the death of a brother or sister."

Taking that in with a frown, Larry made a faint, almost inaudible, whistling sound. The priest noted the reaction and said firmly, "That's how it is, my boy. I'm not going to soften it. But you can write to your immediate family, and receive letters from them, four times a year. Oftener only if there's a serious illness, or a death, or some such crisis. You can't communicate with anyone else outside the monastery, and your parents can visit you only once a year. You sever your previous ties—almost all of them—and this becomes your world. You become part of this community, and together we live for God alone."

He eyed the boy narrowly. He seemed to be taking it in stride. The priest picked up a booklet on his desk. "Let me read you something," he said. Turning to a certain page he read aloud:

> It is quite true the life is hard. Perhaps there is no more exacting rule in the church today; no stricter fasts, no more complete silence, or harder labor. A vowed obedience governs every instant of the day, and says where a monk should be every moment, and what he should be doing. There are no recreations whatever. The diet is so restricted that the community never tastes meat, eggs, or fish; and for part of the year is even deprived of milk and cheese. The monk's only personal privacy is confined to a bare cell and the limits of a small box in the scriptorium in which he keeps a couple of notebooks, perhaps a library book (spiritual reading), and a letter or two that he had not worked up courage enough to destroy.

Then paging farther back in the booklet he read on:

The mortal human life of man on earth is a life of labor, of conflicting desires and appetites, a life of unrest and dissatisfaction, multiplicity and change. Contemplation reduces all this to unity—the unity of one desire, one activity, one striving, the love of God. And by bringing unity and simplicity into our lives, contemplation brings us rest, tranquility, peace. But paradoxically there is only one way to this . . . and that is the cross, sacrifice. For all our conflicting appetites can be quieted only by *being put to death*.

Handing the booklet to Larry he said: "For the first two years, you'll live with the novices. There are eight or nine of them now. They live in a kind of barn, where there's no heat. Their beds are straw mattresses laid over planks. They go to bed at 7 P.M., and their day begins an hour or two after midnight. Bathing is allowed only once every two weeks. They sleep in their burlap—and their blanket of stale perspiration. The odor of the barn isn't always pleasant. But," he said with conviction and no apparent irony, "you'll probably look back on those as your happiest years."

Dear God, Larry thought, what must the rest be like?

Having painted this glowing picture of monastic life, the priest asked, "Are you still interested?"

Larry had heard most of it before. He said calmly but with no counterfeit eagerness, "Yes, Father." Then he made bold to ask a question that he had wondered about before the retreat and more during it: "What percentage of those who enter the monastery actually stay?"

"About four out of five remain."

Larry found the high rate encouraging but also surprising. Almost incredible. He then forced himself to ask a question that he knew might make him seem weak and irresolute but which he had to have answered. He put it hypothetically: "What should a man do if he's in the monastery for a while—say, a year or two— and he finds he's unhappy. Even miserable. And his low spirits just don't go away?"

The question didn't faze the priest. "That's not unusual," he said. "The immediate objective of the Trappist life is not happiness. You know that when you come here. I think a man like the one you describe should persevere in his vocation."

Humph! Larry thought. In that view, "vocation" is a term exceedingly hard to define. Once having entered, if happiness or misery don't matter, by what criterion might one decide to leave? None was apparent. A vocation was assumed to have brought you there, and you should persevere in it. The reasoning seemed oddly—maddeningly—circular. No wonder the retention rate was high. But who was he to challenge the reasoning or judgment of seasoned contemplatives, so revered within the church? You must take a vow of obedience and abide by the decision of your superiors in meekness and humility. You live by a rule (not a vow) of silence. The other vows were poverty, chastity, and stability. Something rebellious in Larry whispered that there must be a *vow of stupidity* in there somewhere. Shocked at his own cynicism, he made an act of contrition.

The priest ended the conference by saying he would arrange an interview for Larry with Father Louis, the master of novices. Larry realized with elation that Father Louis was the Cistercian name of Thomas Merton. He'd had no idea Merton was master of novices.

A personal interview with the great man was more than he had dreamed of. He was almost unnerved at the prospect.

———

It went off smoothly, though. Around one o'clock that afternoon, he was called into the main hall and introduced to a rugged, affable-looking man of medium height with a firm handshake and a disarming smile. His manner was so unclerical and unassuming that it was hard to believe he was a priest, much less a famous author.

First, he proposed going up to Larry's room for their talk, but then decided against it on the grounds that it was "too hot up there." This was such a normal human consideration that Larry was shocked at it. He had supposed the good priest would suggest the hottest place in the monastery as a matter of principle, so they would be in a fitting state of discomfort. But apparently, saintly monks could take liberties in such matters, rest on their laurels, so to speak.

They walked through the monastery garden, out the main gate, and then strolled the tree-lined driveway beyond. The sky was blue and clear but for a few puffy clouds; the sun was hot, the air humid.

"What made you decide to become a Trappist?" Merton asked. He had apparently been assured by the retreat master that Larry's decision had been made.

Larry, taking no chances on a wrong answer, gave him back his own words. "Why live in 'a civilization that is entirely dedicated to the pursuit of shadows . . . for things that you cannot hold on to . . . pleasures that turn sour before you have begun to taste them, and a peace that is constantly turning into war?'"

Merton smiled and said, "I can't take exception to sentiments that are verbatim my own. But many come here expecting a kind of Shangri-la—a pool of warm emotions and a final exit on a rosy cloud."

"I don't!" Larry said emphatically. "I've read the best and the worst of what's been written about contemplative life. It seems to me the bad stuff preponderates, by quite a lot. You live like paupers. Dress in burlap. Labor like peasants. You get up at ungodly hours in the morning. You have long arid periods in your spiritual life. What you wrote about 'infused contemplation' makes it sound like—well, like being lost in a desert. I've read *The Dark Night of the Soul*. Does it sound like I expect Shangri-la?"

"No, it doesn't," Merton conceded.

"On top of all that," Larry said wryly, "I hear you can't date or play basketball."

Merton laughed heartily.

"The truth is," Larry went on, feeling more relaxed, "I don't even especially *want* to enter the order. I feel it's something I *have* to do. That it's the best way of serving God, and—he wants me here."

The monk seemed pleased by this comment, but not wholly pleased. He thought Larry's low expectations preferable to very high ones. Better to come anticipating nothing and find a little, than to seek ecstasies and find the harsh facts. He motioned to the side of the road, and they sat down in the thick grass under a shade tree.

"It's good that you're not expecting Shangri-la. But a little enthusiasm wouldn't be bad, either. This isn't a concentration camp. It's a very healthy life. You always have enough to eat. You get plenty of exercise." Motioning to the green, rolling fields and groves of arching trees, he said, "The surroundings are beautiful. You work hard, but it's often out in the fields, where it's a joy to be. You have lots of time to pray, worship, read, think—contemplate. You live a God-centered life, and everyone around you is living it, too."

Larry replied, "I like all those things, Father. But I'm not leaving home to find something better. Home is wonderful. If I become a Trappist, it's because this is the best way to save my soul. The best way to live as if God is what I'm here for, whether it makes me happy or sad."

Merton looked at Larry while he spoke, then shifted his gaze meditatively inward. "As long as you love God and do his will," he reflected, "that's all that concerns you. Don't worry about the rest, even if it's your happiness." This was a theme that occurred often in his writings, and he enlarged on it. He spoke with a simplicity and conviction Larry never forgot; it was so plainly the story of Merton's life.

After they had talked about various things, the priest discovered that Larry knew no Latin. He explained that a minimum of two or three years instruction in that language was required before one could enter as a postulant for the priesthood. No such courses were offered at the monastery. He suggested that Larry take the courses at home and then enter in a couple of years. Larry made it clear that this was out of the question. He was sick of feeling like a bird under water or a fish in the sky—he had to find his element and find it fast. If he went back to the world, it would be as a worldling. He couldn't drag on in his present state for another month, much less two years.

"Can you sing?" Merton asked.

"Like a frog," Larry admitted.

The monk smiled and said, "A priest spends almost four hours a day in choir singing Gregorian chant. If you're going to sing for four hours a day, you may as well have some fun while you're doing it." Larry was surprised and pleased to hear this ascetic speak of having fun, though a distinctly ethereal kind of fun.

In view of Larry's vocal limitations, his linguistic limitations, and the limitations of his patience (determination to make a move *now*), it seemed advisable to enter as a lay brother. They didn't have to know Latin. They labored more, prayed less, and didn't have much in the way of status, but it was a good life all the same.

"How are you at working with your hands?" Merton asked.

Larry grimaced. "I'm better at singing," he confessed.

Merton laughed and clapped him on the back. Rising to his feet he said, "We'll fit you in somewhere, lad."

As they ambled back to the guesthouse Larry felt a surge of affection for this man that was not unmixed with awe. Sitting in the grass and listening to him talk, a quietness had crept into the boy and a thick knot of tension had unwound. Merton was a holy man who had escaped the affectations of piety. His religion was a masculine thing—strong, virile, muscular—that did not require posturing to make itself felt. He didn't have to flex his virtues to make them bulge under the folds of his cassock. The robust contours of goodness were plainly there, unselfconscious, unobtrusive. Quite possibly he was a saint.

For an hour or so after their parting, Larry was buoyant, as if a ponderous block of misgiving and doubt had suddenly been lifted from his soul. He was confident that if this new life brought him into daily contact with Father Louis, he could bear its hardships. For the first time, he tasted the joy of discipleship, the safety and solace the apostles must have known sitting at the feet of Christ. But of course, Father Louis did not set himself up as a messiah. He did not want a band of disciples and would not welcome idolatry. No interpersonal relationship could be the object of the contemplative life. Had not Merton himself written, "Nothing that we can know and nothing that we can enjoy or desire with our natural faculties can be anything but an obstacle to the pure possession of Him as He is in Himself"? A feeling of devotion for any person would be a distraction from the pure dedication that a monk owed to God.

Besides, there were practical reasons why Father Louis could not play an important part in his life there. How many monks were in the monastery? How many young men were clamoring for his attention every day? At best, Larry would be one among many, holding out his soul and elbowing his way to the front like a schoolboy in a throng of autograph seekers. Merton had his own life to live and his own solitude to nurture. He was so prolific a writer, it was surprising he found time to discharge his official duties. And there was a huge administrative barrier: Larry would be a lay brother, and Merton was master of only novices who were to become priests. Larry would be under someone else's guidance, a man named Father Jerome.

Well, maybe having no Merton connection was best. The love of contemplative solitude is a major reason for withdrawing from the world. "God Alone" is inscribed in stone on some wall of the abbey. Deifying a godly man would be a sin and a hindrance. Merton might be Christlike, but he was not Christ. I must come for God, Larry reminded himself, not for a charismatic man who writes of God.

Pious as those reflections were, he felt the heaviness steal back on him, the contraction in the stomach, the sickening tightness around the heart. An hour after the meeting that had ended so hopefully, his spirits were as low as they had been before.

At four o'clock in the afternoon of that last full day of the retreat, the guests were taken on a tour of the monastery. When they had gone a short way, Larry lapsed into such dour depression that it was hard to be observant. He felt a leaden weight of forlornness and disillusion. Yet some details stayed with him. He recalled the little teenage monk who acted as their guide, sallow faced, freckled, and bashful to the point of stammering when he was questioned: a pitiable stripling who had, it seemed, been wrenched untimely from his mother's arms. There was a large memorial stone where a woman was buried. Having endowed the order generously, she was the only one of her sex ever interred within the walls of a Trappist monastery.

He remembered the small crooked crosses that marked the graves of the monks, so pitifully bedraggled and anonymous looking. He recalled the refectory or eating hall, where there were long wooden tables stretched row after row across the room. The places were set with crude, worn-looking wooden spoons, forks, and bowls. One monk was going from place to place, ladling peach halves out of a crude wooden bucket that most housewives would not have used for garbage; he seemed unaffected by it.

Then there was the large Chapter Room, where the benches were arranged in a quadrangle facing an open space in the center of the floor. Here the community gathered for discourses on discipline, and individuals were reprimanded publicly for breaches of the Rule. Gloomy admonitions from St. Benedict were printed in portentous black letters nearly a foot high around the top of all four walls.

Outside, he remembered the handsome, broad-shouldered, sunburned monk of about twenty-five who was busily clipping a hedge. He turned and nodded to them, smiling, friendly, and to all appearances quite happy. Larry wanted to engage him in conversation, but of course, he was bound by a rule of silence.

In a large factory building, the monks processed and canned produce from the monastery fields. The working monks who filed in and out of the factory were a motley-looking bunch, with no uniformity of age or attire, some wearing baggy rolled-up work pants, others dungarees and old shirts, still others the burlap robes. They made grotesque-looking comments to each other in the sign language as they passed. He remembered a couple of bent-up old men with battered slouch hats, looking as ragged and unkempt as day laborers on a local farm. Their faces were wrinkled, grumpy, and cantankerous; they looked to Larry like any lonely old men whom no one cared about and who cared about no one. They seemed especially forlorn to him since their generation would have passed away almost entirely. To have no one outside the gates regretting one's absence seemed inexpressibly sad.

For the first time, Larry began to appreciate the value of blood relationships, which had always seemed an annoyance in the world, a formal Sunday-visit sort of thing. But here he realized how quickly even the closest friendships would be forgotten. Friendships were active things, a matter of participation, shared experience, communication of feelings and viewpoints. Nothing was more vital and gratifying in a normal life; but let them lapse for years with the knowledge they would not be renewed, and they would dissolve. Like other living things, unless nurtured they would die.

In five years, he could hear his closest friends saying, "I had a buddy in high school. Guy named O'Toole. Went into a monastery. Wonder what became of him." But in five years when someone said, "I have a cousin (or a brother, or son, or nephew) who's a Trappist . . . ," that *meant* something. The relationship was an enduring thing—not vital perhaps, or intense, or fervent, but immediate—and as real as the blood that coursed through their veins. The five-year-dead friendship was only a half-buried shell of recollection. Larry would always be a living actuality to his parents, always an important factor in their emotional lives. They would not forget him in a hundred years; he was surprised to find that so solacing.

He began to appreciate them to such a degree that their sorrow at his leaving began to weigh on him almost as much as his own. His mother was a moderately religious woman. She preferred that he marry, but she could have adjusted to his becoming a secular priest, working in a local parish. She'd have attended some of his Masses, followed his clerical career with active interest. He could have made visits home, joined them for dinner on holidays, coordinated his vacation with theirs. He'd have remained part of their lives and had a visible life of his own. But entering the Trappist order was fearfully like dying. They would never see him again under normal conditions; he was going away and would never come back. When they died, he could not attend their funerals. It was as if *he* had already been buried.

But for Larry, there was no compromising. The secular priesthood did not attract him. He thought it too tame and conventional—a middle ground between the soaring elevation, the wintry peaks, of contemplative life and the flatland on which lay Christians dwell. He was at the foot of a mountain, eye fixed on its icy summit. He would either commence a great ascent—or join the multitudes on the happy plains and beaches of the mundane. He could not, as others did, see the middle ground as a golden mean.

On the last morning of the retreat, Larry was called in for a short interview with Father Jerome, who was in charge of lay brothers. He was a huge man, six feet five inches tall and well over two hundred pounds, solid and nobly proportioned. Now in his late thirties, he looked like a veteran fullback in the National Football League. He had a well-shaped head that was just a bit too small for his body; his features were rough-hewn but pleasing. His handshake was as powerful as his whole bearing promised it would be. He radiated energy and enthusiasm, and it was difficult to imagine him sitting still long enough to contemplate anything. But a contemplative he was, and he had risen to a position of some eminence among his peers.

He pulled over his chair so it was directly facing Larry's and sat on the edge of it, leaning with his forearms on his knees, like a boxer waiting for the bell. One expected his voice to boom like thunder, but he was unusually soft-spoken. Having sized up Larry as an athlete, he asked what school he had gone to and what sports he had played. Larry said his favorite sport was basketball, but with 750 boys in his class—2,300 in the all-boys school—you had to be almost NBA caliber to make varsity. He loved to play but was not highly gifted. Interclass ball was the best he could do.

He sensed that Father Jerome liked him, despite his modest athleticism. He suspected too that he was more . . . well, regular, and prepossessing in appearance . . . than a lot of applicants. He admired and warmed to the man instantly, felt like calling him "coach." But Larry was unpleasantly conscious that in addition to being the Jack Armstrong All-American Boy type, he was also another type this coach would not have liked. He was not uncomplicated enough to adjust as Father Jerome had, with his cheery world-beater exuberance, to the severities of monastic life. If he managed to do so at all, it would be after a psychic trauma that this good man would never understand.

Larry knew his natural personality was not strong enough to run this gauntlet without a miracle of grace, of divine help. He was too delicately strung inside, too sensitive, and with sensitivity went a measure of weakness and susceptibility to pain. It would be the great lament of his youth that he did not have a sufficiently Spartan interior. He was too introspective, minutely aware of every inward vibration. Prone to stumble emotionally over trifles that others take in stride. He despised himself for this, considered it a blight on his manhood. Though he felt a sense of proportion developing, and was much stronger at seventeen than he had been at fifteen, he was still ruefully weak. And until time, or some moral cataclysm, reorganized the structure of his soul, he would be more comfortable under the guidance of Father Louis than under the coaching of Father Jerome.

He left, nonetheless, with the understanding that he would be back in a week, and Father Jerome would be his mentor. The businessman he had met the first night accompanied him on the train to Louisville. They had become friendly the last few days and had discussed Larry's intentions. When they parted at the Louisville station the man said:

"It's a hell of a tough life, Larry. I wouldn't even think of it myself. But you have what it takes. Just knowing you as briefly as I have, I can tell that." Then, smiling, he added, "Maybe next year, you'll say hello to me in the sign language." He shook the boy's hand, wished him luck, and went his way—after which Larry felt more guilty and committed than ever.

The issue had been decided and all the arrangements made, but Larry still could not imagine himself in the situation. Having his hair shaved off, wearing a burlap cowl, living in a barn, never talking, never seeing a girl, never coming home again. These were things you woke up from, things that happened to other people. Yet he knew in his cognitive mind—as distinguished from his imagination—that he *was* entering the monastery and that once he had, nothing short of a nervous breakdown would make him leave.

During an hour layover at Washington, he passed the time by strolling through the airport. In the window of a travel agency, there was a poster showing a smiling, suntanned man and woman in bathing suits. They were tossing a beach ball beside the ocean at some resort. Larry realized with a pang how impossibly remote happiness had become for him. Why was it so? Of all the people he looked at, and he could see hundreds from where he stood, why was Larry O'Toole the only one to whom that picture of simple pleasure seemed as inaccessible as the planet Saturn? Why must fun and romance have no place in his life? What had put a wall between him and sunlight? Why had he, of all this multitude, been singled out for darkness?

When he got off the plane in Philadelphia he saw his mother and Nick Bruni waving to him from the reception platform. He had never been so glad to see anyone in his life. Nick had taken a half day off from his summer job to meet him; never again did Larry value a friendship as he valued Nick's at that moment. Whenever in later years their paths diverged, he would remember that June day and that expression of regard. "There is a friend," the proverb says, "that sticketh closer than a brother" (Prov. 18:24 KJV).

As he got to the top of the escalator, he shoved his suitcase aside, bent down, put his arm around his mother and accepted her kiss on the cheek. Then he exchanged a long bone-crushing hand-shake with Nick.

Larry's mother was a brunette with a trim figure who dressed smartly and managed to look much younger than her fifty years. She had missed being pretty, but with cosmetic art and sartorial care she maximized her assets and was thought attractive. She radiated warmth and the word "effervescent" was often used to describe her personality. But she was not her radiant self on this occasion, when fear of losing her only son was a lead weight on her spirit.

"Have you had enough of that horrible place?" she asked, trying to elicit the desired answer.

"I'm going back in a week," he said.

Her face clouded miserably. "Why did you bother coming back, then?" she asked, half irritated, half in jest. "I'm sure you'll be home by the end of the summer, anyhow."

Larry thought this a bit harsh, then realized she had blurted out the first thing that came into her mind to avoid tears. She was determined not to let him feel committed, to show that nobody was taking the thing seriously.

"I'm sorry to hear that, Larry," said Nick, who had one hand on his friend's shoulder and was carrying his suitcase with the other. "Hell, drive-ins won't be the same, going single."

"I think you've gotten used to the front seat at this point," Larry said. It had been months since they'd double-dated.

Shifting to more serious ground, his mother asked what the monastery had been like and if he had seen Thomas Merton. Though she had come to view Merton as the enemy, she was impressed to learn that Larry had spoken to him privately for half an hour. He tried to describe the man, found he couldn't, and ended by saying simply that he was not a disappointment. His account of the monastery was deliberately and selectively positive.

"There was one disappointment," he said. "I won't be able to become a priest. I've had only a year of Latin and I've forgotten all of it. You can't become a priest if you don't know Latin. So I'll have to be a lay brother."

His mother was furious. To give up the whole world and not even have in return the dignity of priestly ordination seemed the final outrage. "Because you don't know Latin!" she exclaimed. "How utterly absurd! As if God demands that his saints be linguists—especially those who take a vow of silence! Can't you buy a book and learn it? How much Latin do you need to say Mass?"

"Ours not to reason why . . ." Larry shrugged.

"Then why not go to college for a couple of years and get your Latin credits?"

"That I won't do, Mother," he said. "No more waiting. I'm going in now."

After dropping Larry's mother off at home, the two boys went for a ride. Larry felt like he was taking his last look at the old world and he wanted to take a good one.

"Will you be allowed to have visitors?" Nick asked.

"Only my immediate family. And only once a year."

"I'll sneak in from time to time," Nick vowed.

The car radio was playing a popular song in which a velvet-voiced siren implored Larry to abandon his frigid idealism for her voluptuous embrace. He was sure Satan himself had written that song and aimed it at his most gaping vulnerability. He closed his eyes, hummed the refrain, and remembered his last blissful night at a drive-in. He looked at Nick for a minute and reluctantly asked, "Have you seen Mary lately?" It was a subject they generally avoided.

Nick said no, after a slight hesitation. He knew, but didn't mention, that she had been dating a handsome college sophomore with a new Olds convertible. His emotions about Mary were mixed. He tended to regard her as unfaithful to Larry, but he knew full well that Larry had dumped her. The fact that he had dumped her not for another girl but for God seemed an extenuating circumstance that should inspire patient waiting and hope for a reprieve.

The day Larry arrived home from Kentucky was a Friday. That night, Nick dragged Larry to the Wishing Well, a local dance they often attended. Nick hoped a room full of pulchritude would have a salutary effect. For two hours, Larry moped around in an agony of frustration and ambivalence. At ten o'clock, when he could stand it no longer, he took leave of Nick for the night and drove home.

His parents were waiting for him in the living room, as his father paged through an illustrated folder on Trappist life. Matt O'Toole was a fifty-seven-year old businessman who had prospered in both retail furniture and real estate brokerage. He was an eminently practical man, deeply Christian, marginally Catholic. He was inclined to admire Protestant ministers, Protestant preaching, and what he perceived as a more Christocentric faith that focused on Jesus (not his mother and saints) and his gospel of love (less on the sacraments). He attended Mass every Sunday and never considered converting, but his impatience with many things Catholic and admiration for many things Protestant struck his wife and children as subversive.

Just as his mind and personality were a contrast to his son's, there was not much physical resemblance either. Larry, at six foot three, was eight inches taller than the old man. (His five foot three inch mother did not make the divergence more explainable.) Their features were not, if you examined each, very similar, but both men's faces were narrow rather than broad, and a facial resemblance would be remarked on as Larry grew older. The slim, brown-haired, fair-skinned, green-eyed youth was often called good looking; the slightly built, blue-eyed, gray-haired father was called distinguished looking. Because of their size difference, Matt often introduced his son as "a block off the old chip." Larry smiled at this but knew, as years passed, that his father was in most significant ways the man of larger stature.

The Trappist-life folder Matt had in hand was put out by the order to stimulate vocations. On the cover was a picture of a hooded monk standing by a still pond at sunset, gazing peacefully at the reflection of the sky in the water. It was a perfect image of bucolic serenity, and under it was written the Latin equivalent of "O Beautiful Solitude."

His mother had a pamphlet that told of various men who had led brilliantly successful lives in the world, reveled in the sins of the flesh and the pleasures of wealth, but who had found happiness at last by dedicating their lives wholly to God in asceticism and self-denial. Only in the blessed quietude of a Cistercian abbey did their souls discover "the peace that passeth all understanding." It went on to describe a contemplative saint who had been transported by spiritual raptures for hours at a time.

His father pointed to that pamphlet and gestured with restrained emphasis. "Larry, there's ... *falsification* ... here. I don't want to speak disrespectfully of the Trappists, but they . . . lure young men in . . . by promising ecstasies and delights that no practical man can believe in."

"Larry, he's right," Mae declared. "You can't be taken in by this."

Larry's face registered astonishment. He almost laughed.

"Believe me," he rejoined, "a life of enrapturement is not what I expect. Spiritual ecstasies are nowhere in my thinking. The books that influenced me, those by Merton, hardly even mention such things. And when they do"—he reached for a word—"they deprecate them. They talk about how hard the life is. They use the word 'arid' a lot, to make it sound like a desert . . . a desert of the soul. 'Desolation' is another word they use when they talk about . . . spiritual advancement. It almost sounds like the higher you rise toward God, the harder it is to be happy." He excused himself to get a book from his room.

Back a moment later with Merton's *Seeds of Contemplation* and a notepad, he turned to a page in Merton's book first and began to read:

> The ordinary way to contemplation lies through a desert...
> away from vision, away from God, away from fulfillment
> and joy. It may become almost impossible to believe that
> this road goes anywhere . . . except to a desolation full of
> dry bones—the ruin of all our hopes. . . . [M]ost . . . refuse
> to enter upon its burning sands. . . . (153)

"And the desert image isn't the worst," Larry explained. "When you get to the very top—the pinnacle—of spiritual progress, there's something mystics call 'infused contemplation.' That's when the soul gets closest to God.

"I don't have the book here," he said. "It was one I picked up in the monastery library for people on retreat. I jotted down these two sentences: 'In infused contemplation the soul is most intimately exposed to God. One undergoes a scorching of the spirit that is likened to the effects of pure unfiltered sunlight on a diseased eye. It causes pain and a sensation not unlike blindness.'

"A scorching of the soul," he repeated, looking directly at his father, then his mother. "'A sensation not unlike blindness.' You'd think intimate exposure to God would feel like heaven, but it feels more like hell."

His parents stared at him dumbly.

To break the silence he asked, "Do you still think I'm expecting raptures?"

"No," his father admitted. "But . . ." He threw up his hands in incomprehension. "If it's as bleak as what you describe . . . *why in God's name would you go?*"

Larry hesitated. Sighed deeply. "I don't actually *want* to do it, in an emotional way. I just feel I have to. I've reasoned it out . . . and it's the only logical course, for me. The best way for me to serve God and . . . work out my salvation."

"In other words," his father said with a mystified frown, "if you get there and find you're not happy, you won't come out."

"No, I won't. At least I shouldn't. To tell the truth," he admitted, "I don't know of any reason that would justify leaving. The retreat master said I should burn my bridges behind me. He said if a man gets there and finds he isn't happy he should still 'follow his vocation.' That means stay right where he is. Frankly, I don't expect to be happy there. That's not why I'm going."

His father became sarcastic. "Then why *are* you going, boy? To 'follow your vocation'?" He shook his head in disgust. "I don't know what a vocation is if it's not the feeling that you like what you're doing and feel happy doing it." For a moment, he looked at his wife in perplexity. "This thing's got me stopped," he said helplessly. "I've never seen such a tangle. There may be some sense in here somewhere, but I can't find it."

She sat back in her chair and gripped the arms firmly. "We still have one trump card," she said, staring fixedly at her husband. "He can't go without our consent. He's only seventeen."

"Now wait a minute," warned Larry. "Don't start playing with that stuff. If I don't go now, I may never go." An avenue of escape had suddenly been thrown open, and it was so tempting, it frightened him. He had never expected them to stand in his way, and they never would have if his motivation had been normal. But this was a freakish thing, and they had to stand in the way of his unhappiness. He remembered stories about people who started out to live holy lives, but for some reason refused God's grace and became great sinners. Vocations were like flowers, he had been told, delicate things that withered easily, and if you didn't tend them they would die. He knew there had never been a vocation more fragile than his was at that moment. And he was afraid.

"Listen, I'm not very strong right now, so don't tempt me." It was awfully hard to plead against himself, but he made the effort. "I just want you to know the responsibility you'll be taking on. This is a critical point in my life. If I don't go into that monastery now, I don't know where I'll go from here. I feel like anything might happen."

His mother leaned back in her chair. "This is a new turn," she said to his father. "He's liable to blame *us* if anything goes wrong later on. Even if it's an unhappy marriage, or something we can't control."

For a terrible minute, Larry was afraid he had won.

"Then that's a chance we'll have to take," said his father decisively. "I'm not going to sit here and watch that boy throw his life away. Bury himself in a tomb somewhere out of a sense of duty. He doesn't go if he needs *my* consent. Tomorrow, we're writing a letter to the monastery telling them they can have him when he's twenty-one, but not before. I think he'll have straightened a few things out in his mind by then."

He paused for a minute and regarded Larry. "Well, boy," he said, "looks like you're with us for better or worse. You've got four years ahead of you. That's a long time to think things over. I hope you make the best of it."

"And don't be afraid of a little happiness, Larry," said his mother softly. "There are worse things that can happen to you."

"I guess there are," he smiled. Then shrugging his shoulders: "Looks like you call the shots. Fourth commandment and all that." Then he sighed and shook his head. "I just hope to God you know what's best. Because I've reached the point where I don't."

"We don't ever know for certain," his father said. "That's part of being human. There's a risk involved in everything we do. Your mother and I haven't outgrown being human . . . and fallible. But right now we have a responsibility for you. We have to discharge that the best we know how. Maybe we're right, and maybe we're not. We'll just have to wait and see."

"I guess we will," Larry nodded, gazing abstractedly at the floor. "And take what comes. I have to figure out whether you're blocking God's will for my life—or whether he's expressing it through you."

"I'm glad you can see the latter possibility," said his father, rising from his chair. "It's been a long day. We can all use some sleep."

"Good night, Larry," his mother said, kissing him on the forehead. "It's good to have you back."

For a long time after they went up to bed, Larry lay stretched out on the living room floor, staring blankly at the ceiling. He had had a moment of elation, but it passed as quickly as it came. He knew he should have felt relieved or frustrated, but he didn't. He felt numb, just numb. That morning, he had been unable to believe he was actually entering the monastery. Tonight, in a slightly different way, he couldn't believe he was not. It seemed incredible that it was all behind him. Depression—a feeling of gloom about present and future, a sense that pleasure and fun were wrong—had become so much a part of his life that he was afraid to let go of it. Or maybe he couldn't let go; it stuck to his hands.

He should have whistled and sung, he should have laughed, he should have cried. But he was numb. And maybe he was wrong. Maybe he should have begged and pleaded, gone on a hunger strike, done something heroic. He wasn't up to it. For a while, he wanted to sit back and be mediocre. Let the world spin on its own power and bide his time. In a year or two, things would come into focus. Maybe then—just maybe—he would begin to know what the hell it was all about.

Part 3

My Experience with Atheism, Pantheism, Pure Theism, and Christianity
(God Rediscovered)

My Reasons for Believing in God

In 1970, I was a first-year student at Princeton Theological Seminary, studying for the ministry. In my second semester, I took a course entitled Philosophy of Religion. It was given by Professor Diogenes Allen, the most brilliant lecturer I had ever heard. There were no tests, only a final paper on which the entire grade would depend. The topic assigned was "My Reasons for Believing in God." The reasons could be personal as well as metaphysical.

One student had the temerity to ask, "What if I'm not sure there's a God?"

Without hesitation Professor Allen said, "Then your topic is 'Why I'm Not Sure There Is a God.'"

Emboldened by the first question and answer, another seminarian ventured, "What if I don't believe in God?"

The unflappable professor replied: "Then your topic is 'My Reasons for *Not* Believing in God.'"

These exchanges shocked me and perhaps others in the class. But the Vietnam War was raging, and many with no interest in Christian service were drawn to seminary because it offered deferment from the draft. I wondered if this explained the professor's apparent indifference to whether these prospective ministers were believers, agnostics, or atheists. The professor himself was an ordained minister and a devout believer.

What follows—with some revisions and additions—is the paper I submitted to him May 1, 1970, on the topic "My Reasons for Believing in God." I got an A in the course, and the professor wrote on my paper beside the grade: "Thank you for letting me read this document."

That semester was my second and last at seminary. I left because of conflicts between my Catholic past and my Protestant present, which made it inappropriate for me to enter the ministry. But the convictions I expressed in the paper have not wavered since I wrote it.

Many believers are either untroubled by the problem of evil or adjust to it by a reasoning process that doesn't make sense to doubters. In college, I found the problem of evil so unsettling that it drove me into atheism. Then over a period of a decade—ending when I wrote this paper—I moved gradually from atheism to theism and back to Christianity. The stock formulas of Protestant and Catholic apologetics didn't get me there. Some common-sense reasoning did, in combination with insights of great thinkers, emotional traumas, happy accidents, the influence of good people, and, I believe, grace.

This paper gives a brief account of that transition. It offers a way of thinking that penetrates the major obstacle to belief in a personal and loving God. I wrote it when I was about thirty. Now I'm about seventy. That way of thinking brought me out of atheism. And it has gotten me, faith intact, through forty years of confrontations with the problem of evil.

In a confrontation, the horror—whether carnage, agony, death, or grief—glowers at us and says: "Can you look at *me* and still believe in God? You know *I* exist. Don't I prove *he doesn't*?" I may recoil, tremble, and weep. But I can call up the insight, the perspective described below, stare down the horror and say, "I can still see God. You are terrible, but not as terrible as you seem. He can transform and redeem *even you*." I feel impelled to share that insight.

chapter 14

The Rocky Road to Faith

I am not as rigorous as Descartes. This paper presupposes that I exist and I offer no proof of that happy fact, except that I rejoice in it. I laugh, therefore I am. But I don't always laugh, and there are times when I grimace, curse, groan, and shed tears. The universe is a splendid host one moment and an antagonist the next. A caress may turn without warning into a practical joke. A pat on the back may precede a knife in the ribs. And the wine of success—if ever tasted—may smack of vintage arsenic.

Still more dire are the crushings, burnings, starvings, and amputations that bleed and scream across the earth. In short, the problem of evil confronts me at so many turns that I cry out for help. It is the business of this essay to discuss whether such outcries are (a) rational, (b) helpful, (c) heard. Since I have referred to my existence as a "happy fact," the reader has a clue to the final answers.

Emotional Reasons for Unbelief

For eight years of my life, I took pride in not crying out and maintained there was no one to cry out to. The problem of evil vexed me as much then as now, but I viewed it as disproof of the very salvation it made me crave. If there was a God with the power and inclination to get me out of all this, the mess would never have happened. Undeniably, the argument has weight—no more then than now. But I liked it better then because it served my emotional purposes:

(a) I wanted to be a novelist and, in the twentieth century, one's art is gravely hampered if he views the great human drama as choosing between heaven and hell, sin and virtue, God and Satan. That theme was all right in Dante's time, but I doubt Hemingway could have become famous with it, and in my humility, I thought myself a shade less able than he.

(b) To one who had always been a Roman Catholic of the pious sort [if you read Part Two of this book, you know I nearly entered a Trappist monastery at seventeen], there was an exhilaration in reading secular philosophy and a sense of wild adventure in sailing out of the old harbor of faith and onto "the bold sea, with cunning sails" (Nietzsche's phrase).

(c) How can a young romantic, in quest of art and romance, hope to find them if he's worried about smudging up his chastity? Religion had its compensations, but they looked pallid next to Hemingway's experience with a certain lively nurse. That nurse was not necessarily easy to find, but I knew she was out there. Her image was far brighter than God's in my mind, and the thrill of knowing her replaced any vague notion I had of a beatific vision. (I was too ambitious to marry, so there was no hope of combining the ideals. I had to choose between them.)

Religion without God

At age twenty, I changed my religion from Catholicism to the passionate pursuit of a secular trinity: art, philosophy, and beautiful women. That isn't empty rhetoric. True, I became an atheist; but I adored a new trinity that seemed no less divine than God. I worshipped saints (Hemingway, Fitzgerald, Dos Passos, Lawrence, Huxley, Eliot, Voltaire, Spencer, Russell). There were "virgins" who kept my vestal fires burning. And my feelings for all these were religious in the deepest sense. They were my way of coping with existential anxiety. Uniting with them was my idea of paradise, and if I was not a saint, I had my share of mystical experiences. Enough to hunger for more and persevere in the faith.

As the years wore on, the splendor wore off. Maybe the paradise was there and no mirage; but I stormed its gates and could not enter. Salvation depended on my succeeding as a writer. That would have combined the diverse strands of art, philosophy, and romance in a sublime synthesis. But I couldn't pull them together. Beauty and truth seemed sterile things if I could only perceive and not create them, if their grace could flow into me but not out again. I found fragments of romance, and the elusive nurse made her appearance. But to realize the full scope of the dream, I would have had to be a saint in my own right. For only saints can enter paradise.

When the limbo of aspiration became a hell of frustration, I lost my religion. Only a barren atheism was left to me. I tried to fill the void with Hinduism and Buddhism, and for a while they seemed to work. ("to work"—notice my budding pragmatism.) They were so exotic, empirical, unhistorical, and—at least in the Western sense—unmetaphysical, that I could indulge in them without blushing. The God of Abraham would have been a great embarrassment: apart from his lack of sophistication and plausibility, he had too much blood on his hands. I really couldn't be seen with him.

Buddha was a sterling fellow, and you could take him anywhere in Manhattan. He was presentable and in vogue. As an ex-Christian, I was always a little dissatisfied with him for not being divine—but nobody's perfect. He had lots of practical ideas about pulling one's self together, and there were twelve good reasons for following him: the Four Noble Truths and the Eightfold Path. Yet I wasn't enthralled with where he was going. Nirvana (the extinction of selfish desire; enlightenment) sounded like a nice place to visit, but I didn't think I'd want to live there.

The Hindu Brahman (the Godhead, the supreme soul of the universe) was a more luminous destination, a harbor where I might blissfully cast anchor. I had a sneaking suspicion that Buddha, like Columbus, had misnamed the continent he had discovered, and that nirvana was Brahman after all.

Meditations in solitude, in a posture approximating the lotus, were the extent of my practice for several years. I read the Bhagavad Gita, the Upanishads, and some of the Buddhist writings, pondering them and bathing in their mysteries.

Light in Central Park

One autumn day in Central Park, under a tree (not a Bo tree), reading a book called *Practical Mysticism*, I experienced something so like enlightenment, as the mystics describe it, that all other joys seemed like species under that exalted genus. Every vestige of sadness was obliterated, the prison of self was shattered, and I sat with no bars or walls around my consciousness, suddenly entranced by every amber leaf and stone and tree, by the physical book I had been reading, which was itself more fascinating than any thought it contained, by the sunlight and the cool air and the glistening lake. But the leaves I remember best, the leaves and the book.

They were so lovable, and so profoundly real that I seemed like a shadow next to them. No, I wasn't next to them: for that moment they were me, and I loved them as myself—but more joyously than I have ever loved myself. Oh God, what a burden I was freed from then! Nothing could hurt me—because I wasn't there. I was everywhere, I was everything, I was everyone. The book felt smooth and infinitely surprising. Why had I never seen it, touched it before? The leaves were pure enchantment. I caressed them as if they were my bride. It seemed like I had married the world, and it was our wedding day.

The drivers of passing cars were not flitting colors on the landscape; they were precious centers of consciousness with whom I felt strangely intimate. How important you are! I thought of that man speeding by, whom I had never seen before and would never see again. How deeply I understand you, in all your incompleteness. Rich patterns of pain and pleasure vibrate in you now. How absurd and harmless your egoisms are, how endearing your pretensions. You are sacred to yourself, and so to me. A world discrete. A novel painstakingly composed and dense with life, whose chapters I cannot glimpse. You are beautiful! I cried out silently to the old lady on the park bench, and the young mother wheeling her child, and the girl on horseback, and the man with the cane. You are all delightful children, and somehow you are all me, and I am your father, and I love you.

For the first time in my life, I was absolutely unafraid, though I had never before recognized fear as a concomitant of normal consciousness. But the instant ego vanished, fear vanished also, and love rushed in on me like a tidal wave. My separateness was ended. There was nothing to protect, so my spirit embraced everything. I laughed with the glee of a child and the innocence of a saint. For that moment, I knew how it was to be free. I almost knew how it was to be God (or "Brahman," as I phrased it then).

When the immortal hour was over, I went back to my apartment, exchanged casual words with my roommate, got dressed and went to work. The experience, the vision, the ardor were never recaptured in the intensity I have described—and rarely at all. I was in no way transformed, or morally improved, by what had happened in me. But my memory was profoundly enriched. When I hear someone speak of enlightenment, or nirvana, or Oneness with the All, or union with God, or cosmic consciousness, I have an inkling of what they mean. "And God so loved the world. . . ." Yes, I can imagine it. I have known a particle of his freedom, and of the universal compassion that must have glowed in Jesus, Buddha, and the holy men of history. The phrase "Brahmic bliss" is no longer an abstraction but recalls a certain autumn afternoon by a lake in Central Park.

If that beatific vision (which I have sketched very poorly ten years after the fact) had stayed with me in all its freshness, I would feel I had entered paradise. And I know it is only a crude earnest of what can be. This line from the Bhagavad Gita consoled me once in bereavement and expressed my hope for the afterlife: "In the hour [of death], their whole consciousness is made one with mine" (74).

Was the expanded consciousness I had known a cerebral phenomenon and nothing more? Was the transfigured world I had briefly seen just an odd vibration of brain cells, projected on the landscape? Quite possibly. But like D. H. Lawrence I believed:

> That beauty is a thing beyond the grave,
> That perfect, bright experience never falls
> To nothingness, and time will dim the moon
> Sooner than our full consummation here
> In this odd life will tarnish or pass away.
> ("Moonrise," 59–60)

The reader may find this belief so vague that it doesn't qualify as theistic faith. I would reply that its vagueness was its strength then. A creed that was codified, definite, and formal could (I thought) be pinned down, punctured, and deflated by polemics. But mystical experience was less accessible to the cold hands of rationalism— and less vulnerable. I didn't really give a damn that the philosophers had ruled ecstasy out of court, so long as I had tasted a little and could hope for more.

A Kaleidoscope of Theories

True, I was not a strict empiricist. My experience gave rise to theories. For example, it occurred to me that pure consciousness might exist apart from all bodies, and because it was not circumscribed in any way, it would be infinite. I had learned in Central Park that as soon as consciousness becomes uncentered in self, it turns to joy and love. An infinitely joyous and loving consciousness might be the source of my own—might in fact be the very substance of my own consciousness, though bottled up in this quantum of human flesh. Water scooped from the sea is still the sea.

Consciousness, I reasoned, may likewise be one and not many. Only the containers give it separate shapes and colors, and the containers don't last long. When they crumble, the containers lose their diverse forms and return to the great sea of consciousness. Unity is realized and the appearance of separateness ends. To say it in scholastic terms, the essential oneness was always intact, but it was concealed by accidental division and isolation. When the latter is obliterated, bliss prevails. In short, "Atman [the self or soul] is Brahman [the Godhead]! Let us rejoice!"

The above metaphysic was unashamedly eclectic. I didn't care a fig which part was Hindu, or Buddhist, or Catholic—or whatever—so long as it served my purpose. Even the overtones of Gnosticism didn't bother me. I had no scruples about tossing out reincarnation or reinterpreting nirvana. My only obligation was to myself. If I couldn't find a creed to live by I had to make one—out of whatever sticks and stones would fit together into a shelter and an altar. What I described was only a lean-to, and one of several. I would elaborate the plan, deepen the foundation, expand and brace the structure when I decided which design was most comprehensive and habitable.

The Discomforts of Pantheism

Sometimes the idea of being absorbed into God was unappealing. Personal identity asserted its claims and said, "Perfect me, don't destroy me." Or as certain Hindus have put the point, "I want to taste sugar; I don't want to be sugar." Moreover, the belief in the impersonal Brahman involved what I might call technical difficulties:

(a) The vagueness that was an advantage philosophically was often a great hindrance in meditation and prayer. If you wanted your sustenance only *de profundis*, very well. But you couldn't really *talk* to Brahman about the hundred prosaic incidents, problems, anxieties, and satisfactions of your day. Petitionary prayer was even less appropriate.

(b) Frequent meditation in solitude tends to be introverting, if not connected with something like what Christians call "*koinonia*" (fellowship). There was no community aspect to my Hindu devotionals (except for one brief period). Aside from the disadvantage of cultural isolation, the pantheist—at least the Hindu pantheist—looks for "the beyond that is within." Unfortunately, one is apt to spend a lot of time "within" and not find much "beyond." That is a problem for the Christian mystic, too, but he can more easily visualize God as being *other* than himself. To the pantheist, the problem is to realize that he himself is God, and there is no breach between him and the divine Other; in fact, there *is* no other.

This does not prove that the Hindu theology is wrong or inferior to the Christian. I am merely saying that I have found it involuting, at times, and see less danger of this

153

when one believes in a God who is utterly distinct from one's self (however pervasive his presence and penetrating his grace). Christianity makes spiritual extroversion still easier by directing one's attention to a God who is also a man, with a personal history, a book of adventures and quotations, etc. Relating to Jesus, or to the Father, in prayer is much more like normal social intercourse than any pantheistic counterpart I know of. Stated crudely, Christian devotionals are less likely than yoga to produce mystical experience, but more likely to "get you out of yourself."

(c) My one experience with a yoga society lasted only three months. It was uncongenial for two reasons. First of all, emphasis was heavily on hatha yoga, which stresses physical exercises and contortions. Years of muscle-building calisthenics (and a touch of arthritis) have made me stronger but pitifully unsupple. Rarely has there been a more inept yogi. I was forever falling over with a huge thump when everyone else was perched gracefully on his head, and I could not (to save my soul) bend my foot that last two inches into the full lotus posture. After twelve weeks, I had developed only a mild inferiority complex, and the conviction that Brahman was not worth the candle if I had to (literally) stand on my head to find him.

Another source of irritation was that most of my fellow "yogis" (Americans like me)—even the more accomplished ones—were just there to lose weight. With a few significant exceptions, the atmosphere was as spiritual as a game of touch football.

To avoid embarrassment at home, I had to sneak off to these classes as stealthily as Romans once did to the catacombs. This might have added zest if I had, like them, found a pearl of great price. But under the circumstances, it was just one more abrasion. I mention this to point out again how the character of one's culture can militate against a certain view of God. (Of course, temperamental and even physical peculiarities—like my lack of suppleness—can do the same.) There were *several* good pragmatic reasons why pantheism was not the liveliest hypothesis for me, at that time and place. Yet all other routes to religion seemed barred by the problem of evil (which pantheism didn't eliminate but swallowed whole).

"Man's Extremity Is God's Opportunity"

Some months after I had stopped attending yoga classes, my vague nostalgia for a personal God was galvanized by a situation I couldn't cope with. I needed help, and I needed it fast. No one on earth had the solution; I was sure of that. The problem called for a wisdom and power that were nothing short of divine. Don't be naïve, I told myself. There's nobody up there you can talk to. If there were, this earth wouldn't be such a bloodbath of tragedy and disease. Are you going to bury your head in sweet illusions like every pious ostrich? Come off that stuff. Hang on to your self-respect. Grit your teeth. Stand up straight.

But hang it, I returned, I'm flat on my back. That's the fact I have to face. I can't hack it alone. I'm sick of trying. Even sick of living. If things don't change fast, I'm checking out. Oh, God, I wish I could pray. But how can I pray when I don't believe? Talk to the darkness like a fool? Make an imaginary playmate? Not a chance!

But what if—just *what if*—God exists in spite of all your arguments? What if the problem of evil has some solution you've never thought of? What if Bertrand Russell and Voltaire and all those other geniuses just happen to have been wrong? What then! Why, then I'd be a bloody fool to lie in this pit, starving and groaning, and not yell for help. What if he's watching me go through all this? What if he hears everything I think—even now—and is reaching down his hand, if only I'd have the sense to take it?

Oh, God, I don't believe in you. I think it's very unlikely that you exist. I don't have any faith at all. In fact, I think faith is stupid. But I'm desperate, and I *wish* you existed. I really do. Because if you made me, you'd know how I work, and you could fix what's all wrong inside me. It's such a mess. Such an ungodly impossible mess that I can't even begin to set it right. Oh, Lord, if only you existed! There'd be hope then. There'd be a way out of this dungeon. I have to get out. I can't breathe here. Please help me. I need you.

Observe the process: A pain became a wish. A wish became a hope. A hope became a prayer. A prayer became a tiny whispered answer . . . maybe just an echo of the hope itself. But that brought more hope, and more prayer, and more life to a dead spirit. And with that life, or in that life, or from that life, grew faith.

For maybe half a year, my religion was a pure theism. I've heard it said in philosophy class that theism isn't a religion—or "isn't anybody's religion"—but I don't know of a term that better describes my private creed during this period. One definition of "theism" given by the *Oxford English Dictionary* is "Belief in one God who created and intervenes in the universe." I conceived of that God as a personal being who understands the workings of his universe (including my psyche), who cares deeply about his creatures (especially man), and who is willing and able to guide and aid those who call on him.

William James stated it baldly but not without eloquence. He said there are some who need only feel that "we and God have business with each other; and in opening ourselves to his influence our deepest destiny is fulfilled." This unornamented theism pulled me through the crisis that gave it birth. (I believe, of course, that God pulled me through, but that is an inference I will not insist on.) I continued to pray my doubting prayers, and though on my feet again, I was still limping noticeably.

After six months, another crisis developed that was, if possible, even more grave than the last. At the very nadir of my life, nearly paralyzed by despair, I came across a printed sermon that my father had sent me a long time before. It was one of Norman Vincent Peale's, which for some reason, I hadn't thrown out. The title was "Don't Let Anything Get You Down." I have always been disdainful of clichés and Dr. Peale makes unsparing use of them. Somehow I got past the title. Inside, I came across a preposterous suggestion that Peale had made to a man who was just about as battered down as I was. He told him to put a chair beside his bed at night and imagine that Christ was sitting in it, watching him, and caring for him. I didn't believe in Christ any more than I had believed in God six months before. And the idea of using a chair was ludicrous.

But a drowning man clutches at straws, and I felt myself going under for the last time. With a blush that must have glowed in the dark, I did what Peale had urged. And I prayed as hard as I ever have in my life. The thought of the man Jesus sitting there beside me, understanding my distress, loving me though I despised myself, enough like me to occupy a chair in a drab West Side apartment, yet powerful enough to make a star or heal a leper—that thought was consoling and therapeutic in a way that no pure theistic image could have been. Sickness had stripped away my pretensions and made me as helpless as a child. "Unless you . . . become like children. . . ." Yes, I could see it. When I was proud and sophisticated, there was no room for Christ—in my theology or in my heart. But when life had humbled me beyond every vain illusion, I opened myself to his presence and his grace.

After four or five days, I didn't need the chair any more. I had passed through the crisis—or God had got me through it. I knew that I might just have been praying into darkness, and that maybe no God of any kind had heard me or even existed. Maybe, but I had a sense that power came to me and that I wasn't the only presence in that unlighted room. I may be wrong. I don't *know*. But I *believe*. And I'm willing to stake my life on the hypothesis that I'm right.

chapter 15

The Value
of Faith

What I have given above is an account of my practical—largely emotional—reasons for believing in God. Stated briefly, *I believe because I want to, and have found no compelling reason not to.* (In Chapter Sixteen, I show why the problem of evil is *not* a compelling reason.) Through faith, linked with hope and love, I get the power to live a happy and fruitful life. Those last five words have wide implications. To note a few:

"A happy and fruitful life" involves loving God and loving people, and forgetting one's self to some extent in the process. Christianity is superbly designed to help one achieve these three ends.

We feel more at home in the universe if we're on intimate terms with its owner. Cosmic comfort flows from a religious view of nature, as many lesser comforts flow from the scientific view. (Happily, we don't have to choose between them.)

Each day is, among other things, a new tangle of unsolved problems. The God I believe in helps unravel them, large and small, and often cuts through the most impossibly complex. This may be an illusion, I admit, but until someone proves it so I will enjoy its benefits: optimism about life and death, confidence, and an abiding sense of access to the source of all wisdom, strength, and love.

Opportunities for friendship and encounter abound in every church. Apart from its vertical purpose, to connect the believer to God, a church is a unique *social* construct—a craft designed to convey its passengers through the smooth and stormy waters of human life and deposit them on the shores of paradise. In war and peace, in all happy and sad occasions from cradle to grave, we're in this thing together. And *bringing people together* is as vital a church mission as bringing them to God. We have a shared worldview and an exalted common cause. Even when it feels like a ship in a storm, we'd rather sink convivially than float alone.

The Thin Gold Line

Immortality is a pleasing thought. For myself, I would class it as a fringe benefit of believing. I didn't turn to religion because I was afraid of death, but because I was afraid of life. Death was an anesthetic that would end my pain, and I was often tempted to use it. As Nietzsche said, "The thought of suicide is a strong consolation. One can get through many a bad night with it" (86). Now that I have befriended life, death is a villain—whom God has sentenced and will execute.

The idea of paradise and divine union excites me tremendously. It is only a thin gold line at the edge of my horizon, and I am in no hurry to get there. I'm content to sail in these dark waters, to enjoy what stars I can see, to act appropriately in the moonlight, and to share food, wine, and laughter with my fellow voyagers. But the promise of dawn and glory are as real to me as the harbor of destination to any seaman. The current "here and now" theology baffles me. Did Columbus and his men, on the high seas a thousand miles from any shore, think India "irrelevant" because they couldn't see it? Was talk of India dismissed as "pie in the sky"? I think they must have talked often of India when they were gloomy. That kept them going as much as what they ate and drank.

Of course there were doubters. And Columbus didn't find what he expected. But his brash, unempirical faith in *something great ahead* was vindicated. That same kind of faith, and the hope that sustains it, are wind in my sails.

chapter 16

Defending God from Evil

There is no compelling reason to withhold belief in God. I was a long time reaching that conclusion, and I will support it briefly here. A compelling reason would be logical proof that a being with the traits ascribed to God cannot plausibly exist in this universe as we know it. Such an argument would be strongest if it were based on observable facts that cannot be reconciled with an all-powerful, all-knowing, all-good, and loving deity. This brings me directly to the problem of evil, since it is this class of phenomena that seems most able to support, and most likely to produce, the atheistic position (as it did with me). Let's take an example from Dostoyevsky's novel *The Brothers Karamazov*. Ivan is speaking to Alyosha:

> "There was a little girl of five who was hated by her father and mother, 'most worthy and respectable people, of good education and breeding.' . . . This poor child of five was

subjected to every possible torture by those cultivated parents. They beat her, kicked her for no reason till her body was one bruise. Then, they went to greater refinements of cruelty—shut her up all night in the cold and frost in a privy, because she didn't ask to be taken up at night (as though a child of five sleeping its sound sleep could be trained to wake and ask), they smeared her face and filled her mouth with excrement. It was her mother, her mother who did this. And that mother could sleep, hearing the poor child's groans!

"Can you understand why a little creature, who can't even understand what's done to her, should beat her little aching heart with her tiny fist in the dark and the cold, and weep her meek unresentful tears to her dear, kind God to protect her? Do you understand that, Alyosha, you pious and humble novice? Do you understand why this infamy must be and is permitted? Without it, I am told, man could not have existed on this earth, for he could not have known good and evil. Why should he know that diabolical good and evil when it costs so much? Why, the whole world of knowledge is not worth that child's prayer to 'dear, kind God'!"

[Next Ivan tells of a child who, for some minor offense, was stripped naked and fed to a pack of vicious hounds that ripped him apart before his mother's eyes. Ivan says to Alyosha:]

"Tell me yourself, I challenge you, answer. Imagine that you are creating a fabric of human destiny with the object of making men happy in the end, giving them peace and rest at last. Imagine that you are doing this but that it is essential and inevitable to torture to death only one tiny creature—that child beating its breast with its fist, for instance—in order to found that edifice on its unavenged tears. Would you consent to be the architect on those conditions? Tell me. Tell the truth."

"No, I wouldn't consent," said Alyosha softly. (222–226)

That passage was once my major "text" for atheism. Rarely has the problem of evil been more dramatically stated. Even reading it now, I am stirred to indignation and wrath. Better no God at all, we feel, than one who tortures children, or lets them be tortured. "He's guilty!" our emotions shout, "Guilty and indefensible. No need for a trial. Let's drag God from the courtroom and lynch him!" I am impelled to follow, but as I seize my length of rope, the defense counsel lays a gentle hand on my arm and whispers, "He saved your life. Have you forgotten? He stood beside you when no one else did. You depend on his goodness and his love. Can you live without him?"

I pause, realizing how much of me would die if he did. "That can't matter," I cry, to him and to myself. Then clenching the rope: "It's not what he means to me, but what he did to the child that's at issue. I can't spare him for my convenience. Justice matters more!"

"Then in justice hear his case," says reason, quietly tapping his gavel. "Calm down and weigh *all* the facts before you give your verdict. If the evidence convicts him, he will die. I promise you that. But if there is a reasonable doubt, he'll be acquitted. Let the case be heard."

A Trial for the Ages

The scope of this section does not permit a full account of the trial, which dragged on for months. The defendant remained silent throughout and never spoke a word in his own behalf. Reason was the judge and the sole finder of fact. (When God is the defendant, there cannot be a jury of his peers.)

Reason looked appropriately venerable. If not eighty, he was close to it. He had a head of thin but luminous white hair, which he parted on the left and combed back in a neat, becoming way. The disheveled Einstein look of some elderly intellectuals was not for him. His eyebrows were a deep gray, his eyes dark, fierce, appraising, skeptical.

His thin lips formed a straight, hard line that warned he would brook no nonsense. The broad, faintly aquiline nose presided over a long upper lip and a narrow homely face. Of middle height, his body was frail and angular. He looked suspiciously like the philosopher and atheist Bertrand Russell, who had a known affinity for tribunals, though he was not a jurist or even a lawyer. So of course it could not have been he.

Prosecutor Ronald Pavone was a slender man in his mid-thirties, with a full head of black hair, parted on the side and combed back severely. He was strikingly handsome and vaguely familiar. The oval face, the tight strong jaw line, the full sensuous lower lip, the nose that might have been lifted from a Greek statue, the large dark eyes with long lashes under straight thin brows . . . he reminded you tantalizingly of someone. A celebrity. Probably a film star.

You instinctively doubted that a man so physically endowed could also have a trenchant legal mind and rhetorical skills. But he had both, and with them had made a powerful case. The evidence and exhibits were horrifying—from the carnage and atrocities of war, to the crucifying ravages of disease, to the monstrous cruelties of the Holocaust. His summation was eloquent and damning.

Defense Counsel Oliver T. Bower, a man with thinning blond hair, also mid-thirtyish, was a grim sight. His nose was hugely prominent, twice the normal size, thin as an axe head, and so sharply bent at the bridge that in profile it seemed to break at a right angle. He had hardly any chin: a side view suggested a straight line from the base of his nose to his neck. Hugely beaked and almost chinless he had the look of a vulture—or more charitably, an eagle. His ears were large and stood out like cups.

Worse than his terrible features was the *absence* of features in the middle of his face, the blank spot where his eyes and nose should have converged but didn't. His eyes and eyebrows were so near the edge of his face, they seemed almost on the side of his head. At first, you had to stare at him, but then—apart from regretting rudeness—you turned away because the sight was appalling, like the scene of an awful accident. Here indeed was a man whom nature had treated cruelly.

You wondered if Bower could speak at all. If the face was that deformed, could the brain behind it be normal? But the moment words began to issue from those uncomely lips, the thought of mental incapacity was dispelled. The voice was firm and deep, the sentences clear and well-formed, the ideas cogent, the gestures persuasive, sometimes dramatic. The inner man was as magnetic as the outer man was repellant. Your ears overcame your eyes. In his active courtroom persona, the ugly man was a compelling figure. At times, riveting.

Defense Counsel's Closing Argument

"Let's clarify one thing," Bower argued to the court, standing in front of counsel table and facing reason squarely. "The central issue is *pain and suffering* for which God, directly or indirectly, can be held responsible. The abused child—whom God did not intervene to protect—is only an appalling instance of these. If I can show that pain—physical, mental, and emotional—is not *necessarily* evil, the Defendant cannot be found guilty.

"When we say something is 'evil,' what do we mean? The dictionary gives *six* definitions. They have this in common: What's evil is *extremely undesirable* from a human point of view. Everyone agrees that cancer and leprosy are evils. No one wants them. We're trying to eliminate them. We all wish they didn't exist.

"But when we say they're undesirable from a human point of view, we make their character of evil depend on a variable. If our point of view changes, we may no longer see them as evil. Pain would still be pain, and we'd naturally shrink from it. But from a new perspective, we might not wish it out of existence. We might even see it as desirable, though anguishing, in which case the *abolition* of pain would be evil, and the existence of pain in the world would be good. Is this hard to conceive of? Let me read you a few lines from a biography of Leo Tolstoy." He picked up a book from the counsel table, held it in one hand, and gestured with the other while he read aloud:

> Spiritually he prepared himself for the end and calmly anticipated the moment when the spark of life in his pain-racked body would be extinguished. Sickness he regarded as a positive virtue. "One must suffer a severe illness," he

dictated for his diary at this time, "in order to convince oneself of what life consists: the weaker the body, the stronger becomes one's spiritual development. . . ."

He continued to accept his poor health with cheerful resignation and laughingly told his friends that he had gained so much from sickness that for their own good he wished them all bad health. (Volume 2, 317)

Bower closed the book, laid it on the table behind him, and took a step closer to the bench. "Our point of view," he continued, "is the sum total of what we see to be our interests. If those interests end at the grave, what puts us there against our will must be called evil. And what destroys them while we live is evil, too. Yet convince us that we have something more at stake, and we may revise our judgments radically."

Bower began to stride back and forth before Reason, telling a story and making frequent eye contact.

"A misanthropic farmer is oblivious to his wealthy neighbor's estate—totally preoccupied with his own rocky patch of land. His concerns are bounded by the rickety fence at the end of his property. It marks the limit of his forty-acre world, and he never gives a thought to the fertile paradise beyond.

"But hand him the deed to that glorious estate, with its ten thousand acres of ripening wheat, its fruit-laden groves, its splendid manor house, and he'll gladly see his once-precious forty acres turned into an irrigation ditch for the sake of his new and larger interests. The identical event—the flooding of his farm—would have seemed an unmitigated evil from his old point of view. Now he opts for it eagerly. An extending of his interests has transformed an evil into a good."

The Making of Souls

Bower paused for effect, then went on.

"There was a time in Tolstoy's life when he would not have seen anything desirable in sickness, his own or anyone else's. He would have wished it out of existence. Then his conception of man and of the universe expanded. He saw the visible world connected to invisible realities and pervaded by them. He perceived a spirit in man, more vital and enduring than body, and more encompassing than what psychologists call 'mind.' *Spiritual development* became his major criterion of good and evil, superseding the old criteria of pleasure, health, affluence, power, fame—even the creation of great literature.

"In essence, he agreed with Keats that the world is a *'vale of soul-making.'* And his profound discovery was that *there are soul-making qualities in pain.*

"Let me repeat that," Bower said, facing the bench and making fixed eye contact with reason. "I'm not quoting Tolstoy here, but I see this as the truth he was pointing to, and it's the best way I can phrase it." He held an open right hand upward toward the white-haired judge, as if tendering his insight. "*There are soul-making qualities in pain.* Both physical pain and emotional pain."

He relaxed and began pacing again. "Of course, the discovery was not original. There are traces of it in the oldest religions. And asceticism is still important in Hinduism, Buddhism, and Catholicism." He paused, physically and verbally, as if he had digressed—then picked up the thread.

With great conviction, he declared what I took to be, for him, a truth with deep personal implications: *"Pain is so woven into the fabric of human life that we can't conceive of a worthy human being apart from it.* The most admirable men and women could not have become so without tolerating, even embracing, the kinds of pain that stood between them and what they sought to achieve.

"Moving from ignorance to knowledge, from helplessness to skill, requires a willingness to 'grind it out.' For some, it's high school and learning a trade. For others, it's college, med school, or law school. For the athlete, it's mastering the skills of his sport. For the artist, it's years of tedious learning, grueling practice, painstaking creation, and a high risk of failure and rejection in the end."

Bower faced the court and said in a lowered voice: "For Mother Teresa and her disciples, it was carrying the sick, dying, and abandoned through the foul streets of Calcutta to their places of shelter and healing. Pain confronted, pain endured, and pain relieved— the essence of heroism and virtue." He held the last gesture reflectively for a moment, eyes locked with those of the glowering judge, whose thoughts were indecipherable.

Pacing again, Bower shifted from the sublime to the mundane, and his demeanor became casual. "Consider those milder forms we call discomfort. Teaching a baby to control its bodily eliminations is, in a measure, teaching it to accept pain. This is one of the first conditions of moving from infancy to childhood: to act on motives other than desire for comfort; to please one's parents though it pinches a bit. The seed of soul making is in that elemental fact of human growth. It's pregnant with the morality of our later phases.

"The same is true of walking. A baby's first steps are frightening and usually end in a fall. They're emotionally and physically painful.

Why does she do it? Normally at the constant encouragement of her parents rather than to please herself. (I've heard that small children who grow up abandoned in wild places don't become bipeds.) You might say that a child could advance to that phase even better if there were no pain involved. From a mechanical standpoint, that may be true. But there would be no soul making then, no element of moral choice, no germ of self-overcoming.

"Point out that the child is still acting from selfish motives (her ego is fed by her parents' applause), and I reply: true, but so does the most exalted saint, who loves God because in God he is fulfilled, and his neighbor because only thus can he love God and find joy. Our selfish motives are God's creation and lead ultimately to him—but *we ascend through pain*. Giving is only mechanical if it doesn't hurt a little, somewhere. What makes it spiritual—moral, if you prefer—is the sense of loss at which we grimace inwardly as time or money passes from our hands.

Pain in Virtue, Heroism, and Love

"Without pain and the possibility of more pain, in one's self and in others, virtue could not exist. Human society itself, and bonding between persons, could not exist. If no one could be hurt, no one could be helped. If no one lacked, to whom would we bring our gifts, and why? If no one got lonely, our companionship would be worthless. Whom would we befriend? Whom would we love if no one felt the pangs of incompleteness? We would have no need of love or of loving.

"Why do we talk to each other but to mend our fragmentation in a hundred friendly ways? To make each other less lonely, or less ignorant, or less discouraged, or less afraid? We would all be as stolid and incommunicative as trees but for our common suffering and our efforts to rescue each other from it. We'd be a vast, silent, unmoving forest of men—with only wind between them. No; don't call them men. Call them ferns, perhaps, or oaks, or elms—not men."

Here Bower stepped toward the bench and drew himself up as if to make a great pronouncement. Holding his open hands in front of him, as if drawing a truth from his breast and extending it to the throne of reason, he exclaimed:

"*Pain is a defining attribute of our humanity.* We come wailing from the womb. We approach our final breath 'with fear and trembling,' knowing that in some sense when our pain ends, *we* end. And all the days that pass between those two events are a struggle—heroic or abject—to understand, bear, avoid, alleviate, or triumph over pain in ourselves and others.

"Sacrifice is a voluntary acceptance of pain, to achieve or confer a benefit. Soldiers do it on the battlefield, where the cost may be death or dismemberment. Parents of newborns do it in a nursery, where the cost is merely lost sleep and leisure, discomfort and expense—but years and years of those. The faithful wife gives up other men, the faithful husband other women. The child who would be a pianist sacrifices hours of delightful play and socializing to master an art." Then stressing key words by tapping his right palm with the front edge of his left hand he averred: "*Everything good and admirable in human life involves sacrifice and pain.*" He held eye contact with the judge for several seconds, then broke it and went on pacing out his thoughts.

"We gather to chat, laugh, drink, and share amusements when we're winning, as mostly we feel we are. That's our brave way of coping. But everyone at the table, bar, or cocktail party knows—if only half consciously—that pain of some kind is not far behind her and is lurking ahead, and the same is true of everyone she smiles at or clicks glasses with. It takes many forms: physical pangs, mental anguish, emotional distress, social setbacks, romantic disappointments, financial loss. Death.

"A world without pain would be a world without human life. It would be a world without joy or pleasure, since these are what we experience when we gratify desire. And *desire is pain*, mild or intense. Without the pang of desire, there would be nothing to gratify. A rock feels no pain, so it's incapable of pleasure. Nothing is good or evil to a rock. Those terms are expressions of desire, to have or to avoid. If pleasure is the satisfaction of desire, and desire is pain, then pleasure is grounded in pain—and could not exist if there were no pain. So too with joy and happiness."

Bower paused, looking fixedly at the judge, as if trying to gauge his reactions. Were these arguments registering? The intelligent, brooding, cranky face of reason was an enigma to me, and I suspect to Bower. The old man's attention never wavered, and you knew he understood everything. But as to agreement or dissent, his immobile features gave not a clue. Bower seemed to shrug faintly, then resumed his measured steps back and forth before the bench, his tone now even and matter of fact.

"Every human organization is created to diminish pain. Hospitals most explicitly, of course, and charities. But every business is designed to satisfy a need, and need is a species of pain. People devised government to deliver them from the chaos and trauma of anarchy. Governance may hurt, but anarchy hurts more.

"The undramatic forms of pain are so common we fail to think of them when we speak of the problem of evil. Work is pain, exertion is pain, dieting is pain, charitable giving and volunteer work—*all* forms of altruism—are pain. These have benefits, but we pay for them with pain. In Christian theology, God did not exempt even *himself* from pain—embraced through the Incarnation, with torture and death on a cross."

"Objection, Your Honor!" cried the prosecutor. All turned to the sculptured face of Ronald Pavone. He seemed an apparition from heaven to eyes not yet inured to Bower's hellish features. Pavone had risen to his feet behind the counsel table. "The fantastic claims of theology are banned by rules of evidence in the Court of Reason."

Reason leaned back and fingered his chin. "Sustained," he said, "but I would remind the prosecutor that some license is permitted in a closing argument. A religious allusion can be rhetorical, not evidentiary." He picked up the gavel and announced: "We'll take a half-hour recess."

"All rise!" the clerk commanded.

With a light tap of the gavel, the judge stood, as did all in the courtroom, and exited in a dignified octogenarian shuffle.

During the break, I chatted with a man who sat next to me, also there to observe. He introduced himself as Ben Gold. He was of medium height and bulky build, with brown, wavy hair. His pleasant but undistinguished face was dominated by his upper lip. It had a permanently swollen contour, as if he had been punched, but there was no sign of a bruise, and you could tell it was just that kind of a lip. It spread out and lost its puffiness when he smiled, and he had an engaging smile.

He said he knew Bower and Pavone. Both had been in his law school class. He was not a close friend of either, but they had always interested him. You could not have found more contrasting types. Ron Pavone was the handsomest guy in the school, a fact not lost on female classmates, often heard to lament the fact that he had a gorgeous young wife. Women students found him funny, personable, and harmlessly flirtatious. Some male classmates, with whom he was less popular, questioned the "harmless" aspect of his flirtations and whispered that he was serially unfaithful to his wife. Gold didn't know if there was anything to the rumor. Jealousy would have been enough to account for it. But five of the six students in Pavone's informal study group were women.

Ollie Bower was the loneliest guy in the class. His grotesque facial deformity was not the only barrier to social intercourse with him. He was pathologically shy, incapable of making small talk. He would blush violently whenever Gold tried to engage him. Yet in classroom discussion, he was confident, intelligent, and articulate. Seeing his isolation, Gold invited him to join his small study group. Bower accepted. He was silent during the light chatter, but when it came to talking law, no one did it better. He understood every case, every concept, every theory they had to grapple with. Gold wasn't sure how much of Bower's mastery came from filling the social void in his life with study and how much from a trenchant legal mind. The result, in any case, was impressive.

"All rise!" the clerk bellowed when a half hour had elapsed. Hoary reason resumed his place on the bench and, with a gruff nod, indicated that defense counsel should proceed with his summation.

No Humanity, No Joy without Pain

"Now let's reason to a conclusion," Bower continued. "God is accused of evil; that is, of culpability for human pain. What is 'evil'? It's a term we use to describe what is undesirable from a human point of view. Is pain undesirable from a human point of view? To say so is to say that good character, virtue, and heroism should not exist, since—as I have shown—*every admirable human quality is acquired through pain. Every noble act is sacrificial.* To say there should be no pain in the world is to say there should be no strong, brave, generous men and women, since we can't conceive of them apart from pain. So to call pain evil is to misunderstand its function in human life. To misunderstand life itself." Bower stared at the judge, to let the point register. Then he lowered his eyes and began to pace.

"Do men know that by wishing pain out of the world, they are wishing not only virtue but even *joy* out of existence? Do we understand ourselves so poorly that we fail to see this? We want escape from pain, yet pain is a prerequisite to joy. The thrill of joy is its contrast to pain. Victory's joy is deliverance from the peril and humiliation of defeat. The joy of love is its contrast to loneliness, rejection, or frustration. Wealth is a joy only to those who have felt or feared the sting of poverty. Without knowledge of pain, we could not know joy. And joy is what we seek! Ambivalent, confused, suffering, searching—crashing to the ground, rising with cuts and curses, tenaciously plodding on. That is the human story, pain lined and pleasure driven. So it will always be while we walk this green earth."

I could not help but think that Bower—poor, deformed Bower—*looked* like a man who knew whereof he spoke. A man for whom every mirror, and every face that grimaced when he passed, was an occasion of pain. Yet he had learned to see in pain a creative and elevating function.

"Consider the basic issue, Your Honor. What does it mean to say that God is guilty of evil? It means he has created a human species that is capable of goodness, even greatness! Capable of generosity, high achievement, and love. When you look at pain in that context, it's part of a magnificent design—which would fail without it!"

Defense counsel stared up at reason, who seemed swayed by his arguments yet not entirely convinced. Counsel paused, pondered, then went on.

The Problem of Good

"But I anticipate your objection. Even conceding all I have proven, there is still the little girl, tortured by her parents and locked in the cold privy at night. And there is the little boy, torn apart by the dogs. You can accept the pain of the child learning to walk, and the pang of loneliness we've all known, and the varieties of bearable pain that stab and scar our normal days. You will grant that pain per se is not evil. But you are horrified by the extravagant excesses of pain and suffering that shatter so many lives, that make existence torment for the stricken. Pain is necessary, you say, but why in such diabolical intensity, why in such awful profusion? Here I can only hint at answers. Fortunately, that will be enough, because I need merely show there are *possible* explanations not involving guilt for the defendant.

"Have you ever contemplated *the problem of good*? I'm thinking of persons who have been rendered worthless by insufficient suffering. Take, for example, the spoiled child. His every desire is quickly smothered by satisfaction. The natural effort of pursuit is unnecessary for him. He's denied his minimum requirement of pain, and the result is dehumanizing. He's rude, clamorous, swaggering, petulant, querulous, sarcastic, always compulsively seeking center stage, callous to the feelings of those around him. These unpleasant traits stand out most obnoxiously in a spoiled child, but in any group of children—especially adolescents—they're far more conspicuous than in adults.

"The parents of such children are usually polite, friendly, modest, considerate, and reasonably sensitive to the feelings of others. We dismiss this striking contrast with the word 'maturity,' but that names the difference without explaining it. Let me suggest the cause: the parents have been longer and more nakedly exposed to *the soul-making power of pain*. Children who have been forced to work in mines or factories from an early age (think of Dickens's David Copperfield) show many of the same qualities of 'maturity.' I would emphasize the *spiritual* content of that phenomenon; the physical and chronological aspects are incidental.

"We all know adults who are still, in essence, spoiled children. The pain factor that would have made them otherwise has been absent from their experience—partly due to circumstance, partly due to their own volition. Their souls have been stunted by easy pleasure. This not-uncommon tragedy I call the problem of good. If there were only so much pain per capita in the world as there is in the lives of these spoiled children, the human race would have little to boast of. We would be a planet of petulants."

Was it my imagination, or did Bower cast the briefest glance at prosecutor Pavone, when he spoke of the problem of good? The self-assured Pavone did not seem to notice or take offense.

"I will make my point quickly," said Bower, fearing the court's impatience. "I need only mention Jesus, Buddha, Ignatius of Loyola, Francis of Assisi, Father Damien the Leper, to recall how great quantities of suffering are combined with love to make the most glorious and perfect human souls. I can't account for the agony of infants. I can only say that *every admirable human trait is acquired through sacrifice and pain. And any judgment of what is good or evil depends on the extent of a human being's interests, which may go far beyond what our senses reveal.*

A Moral Universe

"I can't account for the torment of babies, but I couldn't account for my own pain until recently—and now I can."

This was the first expressly personal note to creep into the summation. Apparently Bower's reconciliation to "[his] own pain" had come not early in his life, but late—and probably after great struggle. He went on.

"What human being is sure that he will never reach a higher level of insight than he enjoys at this moment? We've passed beyond so many, why shouldn't there be more? A sage made this astonishing remark: '*The universe is moral to its core.*' Moral to its core! Designed for soul making. That proposition can't be proven by microscopes or telescopes or experiments with matter and energy. But it can't be *disproven* that way either.

"If it's true, pain and its spiritual value can be judged only when we see the *whole* of human existence: life, death, and what may be *its shining Sequel.* There is no agony, however protracted; no tragedy, however hideous; no cataclysm, however earth rending, that an infinitely powerful God cannot redeem. The girl in the cold privy, the boy devoured by dogs—they can both be transfigured, made perfect, whole, and radiantly happy by the Mind and Will that called the galaxies into being, then created the mystery and wonder of human life."

The unsightly figure of Bower had begun to glow. This was the summation not only of his case, but of the hope he lived by.

"The emergence of beatitude from wretchedness was foretold by the author of the Beatitudes: 'Blessed are you that weep now, for you shall laugh.'

"Paul admits in 1 Corinthians 2:9 that it's beyond our imagining: 'Eye hath not seen, nor ear heard, neither have entered into the heart of man, the things which God hath prepared for them that love him' [KJV].

"Yet Paul describes one vital element of our transfiguration: '[T]he Lord Jesus Christ . . . *will change our lowly body to be like his glorious body*'" [Phil. 3:20–21 RSV].

When Bower said "our lowly body," he motioned eloquently to his own. I guess any lawyer would have, but for Bower it meant more. Prosecutor Pavone was growing visibly restive, his face flushed, his fist clenched. He seemed about to speak but restrained himself. Bower went on.

"John in Revelation tells in one verse how the vast ancient drama of human suffering and death will end for believers: 'God himself will be with them; he will wipe away every tear from their eyes, and death shall be no more, neither shall there be mourning nor crying nor pain any more, for former things have passed away' [Rev. 21:3–4 RSV].

"So life and joy, not pain and death, will be the last words of the human story. Paul speaks of—"

"*Objection*, Your Honor!" cried Pavone, slapping the table. "We're patient with rhetorical flourishes in a summation, but this has gone too far. Counsel will read us the whole Bible if we let him. His line of argument is inadmissible. This is the court of reason. An occasional phrase may be tolerated, but whole passages from Scripture have no place in it."

The judge, who had apparently been moved by Bower's oration, glared at Pavone, then saw the point of his interruption. "Objection sustained," he said. "Those quotations will be stricken from the record. Defense counsel will confine himself to logical argumentation and observable facts. No appeals to Holy Writ. He knows the rules of evidence."

Bower bowed to the court. "I stand corrected, Your Honor. Those Bible texts were meant to show *what* Christians believe, not to prove the beliefs are true. I don't have to prove my client's innocence. I need only show that the prosecution has not proved guilt beyond a reasonable doubt. I've established much *more* than a reasonable doubt. I rest my case."

The court recessed, deliberated, and eventually returned with a verdict.

On the ground of insufficient evidence, the defendant, Almighty God, was found not guilty of evil and was acquitted. Those of us who would have lynched him are now wiser if not holier men. If we have not the faith to believe, we have at least the reasonableness to doubt.

After the judge made his ceremonious exit, the courtroom buzzed with conversation. Ben Gold and I chatted briefly about the decision. Then he said, "Come on, I'll introduce you to the lawyers." I followed him to the prosecutor's table, which was closest to us.

Ron Pavone greeted Gold warmly, and Gold introduced me. After they had bantered a bit, Gold said, "I was here for your summation. I've never heard you argue better."

"Thank you," Ron said. "I don't think I ever did argue better. Seemed to me like a winning argument."

"Of course, Bower was good, too," Gold observed fairly.

"He was," Pavone conceded. "He's been a tough litigator since moot court in law school. Bright and eloquent—a tough guy to beat. He puts his heart in it because it's his whole life. That's true of every case, but for him, this wasn't just a case. This was a crusade. He needed the win more than I did. God is all he's got."

Gold looked puzzled. "God is all he's got?"

"You know what I mean. He had no life in law school. You remember that. He has none now. We're in the same high-rise. He still lives alone. His parents are dead. He was an only child. (After *his* misfortune, I guess they wouldn't risk others.) He has no friends, no chance of romance, no kids. Nothing but his work and his religion. This case meant everything to him. A good and loving God is his only hope. He argued like his life depended on it, because it does. At least, his *after*life depends on it."

"And yours doesn't?" I interjected.

"Don't believe there *is* one," Pavone declared, eyeing me with mild surprise. "But my *life* depends on other things." He smiled at Gold and glanced toward the back of the room. "Like them," he said, nodding toward a darkly beautiful woman, who I guessed was his wife, and their preteen daughter, a stunning reflection of her handsome parents. "I've got to go," Pavone said. "Good seeing you." He shook hands with Gold, nodded at me, and off he went, an admiring female on each arm.

"Well, he's not a sore loser," I said to Ben.

"No, in fact, he's always been a winner. And so are his wife and daughter." He stared after the three in admiration. "Some guys have it all."

He looked around for the defense counsel. "I would have introduced you to Bower," he said, "but he's gone. The world's shyest human. He vanished instantly, the way he did after study sessions in law school. The biggest victory of his career, and he doesn't stick around to socialize or celebrate. The poor man is locked in solitude. He saw me, and nodded once, but he was too shy to come over. While I was talking to Pavone he made his getaway. Now he's off somewhere, by himself, as always."

"Savoring the hope he vindicated," I said, to put it in a kinder light. "Maybe in the company of the acquitted defendant."

"That's a good way to look at it," Gold smiled. "Well, I've got to go. Nice meeting you." We shook hands, and he left.

This brings me to my conclusion.

chapter 17

No Rational Barrier to Faith

There is no compelling reason to withhold belief in God. The problem of evil may be a stumbling block, but it is not a rational barrier to faith. You can get by it if you want to, without violating your intellectual conscience. The fundamental question is, do you want to? The available facts don't carry the day for either side. So you must make your choice. Will you stand with God or with no God? Intellectually, you may be neutral, agnostic, but spiritually, there is no middle ground. God is in your life, or he is not. To ignore him is to reject him.

How should you decide? Well, how do you make any important decision in life? How does a man decide whether or not to marry? He begins by consulting the most venerable of human motives, self-interest. Does the possibility of marriage appeal to him? When he weighs the advantages and disadvantages, does he, on the whole, *wish* he were married? If there is even a faint apprehensive wish, he will experiment with casual relationships. If he has no rapport with a girl on a date, obviously he won't commit his life to her. But if the date diminishes his loneliness, cheers him, helps him forget himself and his problems, he'll go back for more.

Let's say the relationship deepens. He sees the other person as a reality no less complex and interesting than himself. He feels appreciated, understood, and encouraged. The beauty of the other grips his heart, brightens his hopes, and warms his world. Simply and passionately, he falls in love with her and senses that she loves him. When that stage is reached, the decision to marry flows naturally from the existing relationship. He could never have made it in the abstract, sitting in his room on a Saturday night, contemplating a long, bleak line of gloomy Saturday nights but skeptical about the appropriateness of marriage. He does not, in fact, choose marriage at all, but *a person* he has come to know and love.

Your Enlightened Self-Interest

One does not choose religion either. One chooses God—after one has passed through all the stages that lead from doubt and inhibition to trust and adoration. For most of us, they come slowly, phase by phase.

A friend of mine from high school once stated the problem succinctly. He said, "There oughta' be a God, but there ain't." I have tried to establish in this book that nobody *knows* "there ain't," just as nobody *knows* there is. Conceding that, the person who genuinely feels "there oughta' be" has fertile ground for faith. If the ultimate significance of human life is an open question, why not resolve it in your favor? You have to act on one premise of several that may be true. Why not pick the best? Why not base your life on the happiest possible (and plausible) interpretation of the universe? If that includes a God who loves you, embrace at least the idea. Wish freely and imaginatively that he existed. Savor the poignance of the desire. Then reflect on the strong objective possibility—the hard philosophical fact—that God may be as real as the chair you're sitting in, and as close to you.

That being so, it is in no way delusive to *hope* that he exists. The plainest rule of mental health is to hope for the best, rather than fear the worst. Express your hope silently to the God who may hear you. Express any hope you have, or any fear, or pain, or doubt—even about him. Open yourself to his influence. Experiment. Do it often. Imperceptibly, your hope will be mingled with love. In time, belief will draw so near that you can grasp it, if you will. What have you got to lose? What have you got to gain?

That was the mental process that led me to faith.

Shane Hayes
Submitted to Professor Diogenes Allen on May 1, 1970

Part 4

A Shining Sequel
(Her Last and Finest Hour)

A Shining Sequel

In Part Three, "A Trial for the Ages" dealt with the problem of evil from a philosophical perspective. Here in Part Four we go from the abstract to the concrete. The day after my mother died, I wrote the story of her last illness, with no intention of making any kind of moral point. I hoped the *Philadelphia Inquirer* would carry it in the obituary section. Instead, they made it the lead article on their op-ed page. I include it here because, beyond its human interest, there are six scattered sentences toward the end of the narrative that show how differently we viewed her plight as believers from the way we would have viewed it without faith. Those six details transform the story as they did the experience, for her and for us.

Her Last and Finest Hour

"I've had a good life," my mother sighed from her hospital bed, the night before she was moved to intensive care. "I really shouldn't complain." She was struggling for breath when she said it, with pneumonia in both lungs.

And it *had* been a good life, on the whole. Anne Hayes was eighty-two, happily married for fifty-six years. Her husband (my father) was alive and doing pretty well at eighty-eight. She had raised two children and—because her daughter died young—one grandchild. Her home, though modest, was beautiful inside and out, a reflection of her character and her taste. She had enjoyed many summers at the shore, trips to Europe, and an active social life that included much entertaining of family and friends.

She was a person of unusual vivacity and warmth who tended to make an impression on people that they didn't quickly forget. Her former employer had sent her a box of candy on her birthday each year until he died, more than forty years after she had left his employ to marry my father.

Though never beautiful, she had kept a girlish figure into her late sixties and always made an attractive appearance. ("It gets harder and harder," she'd say when complimented in later years.) And she had a self-deprecating sense of humor. She often told of a well-intentioned remark made to her at age sixteen by a boy who was charmed by her warm personality: "Anne, I'd rather go out with you than a pretty girl," he had said earnestly.

The last ten years of her life were a protracted series of broken bones, operations, and painful convalescence. The adjustment was hard: no more trips to town with friends, no more entertaining, no summers at the shore, no travel. And then, when her last illness struck six months before her death, even eating and breathing became difficult.

Usually, in obituary writing, little or nothing is said about the circumstances surrounding death, or even the cause of death. I'm going to violate that rule here because I think my mother's last hour was perhaps her finest.

She was acutely aware of the torment and futility of dying by degrees over a long period, when there's really no hope of recovery. My sister, Eileen, endured that—starved to death over eight months because her body could no longer absorb nutriment from food. My mother had been with her every day of those eight months; watched the girl shrivel to a skeletal fifty-seven pounds before death released her. For both of them, the emotional pain had been almost as searing as Eileen's physical pain.

The ordeal left a profound impression on my mother. "If I get terminal cancer or something hopeless, don't keep me alive," she said. "Don't do anything to stretch it out. Just give me lots of painkiller and let me die." And she said that not just once, but many times.

Her doctor called me a week before her death and said her condition had worsened; they were moving her into intensive care, and he wanted my permission to put her on a respirator, if necessary. She had advanced pneumonia and might soon be unable to breathe on her own. Her mind was not clear enough to make a decision at that point. I agreed reluctantly, on the understanding that it would be a short-term measure to get her over the crisis and see if new antibiotics would reverse the decline.

Within a half hour, they had her on a respirator. It was a grim sight: a tube half the width of a hose stuffed down her throat, pumping sharp gusts of wind into her chest; her mouth wide open, gagging and coughing on the tube; a thinner tube in each of her nostrils and another cut into each arm. She was suffering terribly that first day, and I felt weighted with guilt. "She's in hell," I said to my wife, "and I want her to be in heaven."

The second day, I had the doctor withhold her painkiller long enough for her mind to clear. When her eyes were open and alert, I said, "Mother, I know you hate this tube in your throat, but if they remove it . . . you'll stop breathing . . .and you'll die. Knowing that, do you want them to remove it?" I thought she shook her head, but I wasn't sure. (She couldn't talk, of course, because of the tube in her mouth and throat.) Then my wife Jill, standing beside me, said, "Do you want to go on fighting a while longer, Anne?" My mother nodded; definitely yes.

With heavy sedation, she was awake only intermittently during the next week. Her condition worsened until there was only one chance in ten that she would survive. If she did, she would always have to eat through a tube in her stomach and breathe through a tube in her throat, attached to a respirator.

On the seventh day in intensive care, she was awake and lucid. She managed to communicate to her nurse and then to her doctor that she wanted the straight facts about her condition. The doctor squared with her. Through his questions and her nodded responses, she made it clear that she wanted the tube removed, though that meant she would die. The doctor agreed, and my mother—to his surprise—reached out a hand strapped to a board and tube, and shook his hand to express gratitude. The nurse was in tears; my mother reached out, brushed them away and indicated that it was all right; it was best.

My wife, who witnessed all this, summoned me and my father by phone. We came at once, confirmed with Mother through questions and nods that she wanted the tube pulled, though she knew the almost certain consequences. I asked if she had prayed. By an eloquent expression and an emphatic nod, she assured me she had prayed and prayed plenty. I read two appropriate verses from Scripture ("I am the Resurrection and the Life" and "Today you will be with me in Paradise").

My father kissed her good-bye. Among other things, he whispered, "I'll see you soon in heaven." My mother gave him as much of a kiss as the tube permitted. My wife and I said our farewells. I held one of my mother's hands and my wife held the other, while the morphine made her drowsy. She fought the drowsiness, intensely aware that when sleep came, she would not wake from it. Not in this world.

But sleep did come. We held her hands and stroked her arms and prayed for her—and wept for her—until, four hours later, she had drifted from us—and the doctor said finally, "She's gone."

Gone. My mother, friend, and mentor. She taught me not only how to live, but how to die.

Part 5

How an Agnostic Sees Christ and His Mission

(A Profile: His Life in Nine Hundred Words)

How an Agnostic Sees Christ and His Mission

"Man is born to trouble as the sparks fly upward." Job 5:7

God made his own incarnate experience illustrate that grim insight into the human condition. We tend to think of Jesus' life as having two contrasting phases: three decades of a placid "hidden life," followed by a tumultuous public ministry—the unquiet years. But were there, in fact, any *quiet* ones . . . before the cross, or after it?

He was conceived in a way that so transcended the natural as to seem fantastic, apocryphal, to many—then and now. The news of his mother's pregnancy before marriage must have been jarring to her family, as it was to her fiancé. His birth was ill timed and comfortless. When the king heard about it, he issued his death warrant and slaughtered scores of babies in an effort to dispatch him, while his parents fled the country to save his life.

They ventured home when the king had died, only to find that his genocidal son, who had executed thousands, ruled Judea in his place. So they crept like fugitives to a Galilean village to escape the tyrant's sword. *Born to trouble.*

When Jesus was twelve, his parents traveled to a distant city, lost him on the way back, and commenced a frantic three-day search. They found him not frolicking through streets in adolescent games or mischief, not panicked at being lost or left behind, but in the Temple striving, precociously, to illuminate the Scriptures, and to pierce the veil of prophecies he felt ominously destined to fulfill. He gently reproved them for not knowing where to find him. Was he not his Father's son?

After that, there were eighteen years of which we know almost nothing, so we assume (but should we?) that they were serene and uneventful.

The next three years split history in half. He performed prodigies of healing, spoke with more resounding effect than anyone before or since, and taught radical doctrines about human and divine love.

He made hundreds of powerful enemies and a dozen weak, inconstant friends. His fame crested, enemies seized him, and his friends vanished. He was accused of crimes he didn't commit, brutalized by guards, found innocent despite perjured testimony, yet sentenced to capital punishment, and tortured to death with whips, thorns, and nails on a wooden rack.

They left his torn, lifeless body hanging on the dark hill where they had killed him. They couldn't even let his corpse rest in peace but gashed it open with a spear. At dusk, an admirer summoned the courage to bury him.

But even his loving Father didn't leave him at rest for long. On the third day, with a death-shattering sigh, he breathed life back into him, and he strode from the tomb radiant with inextinguishable light. *One small light that foretold the end of darkness.*

The bliss of heaven beckoned, but he stayed to finish the work he had left undone. No rest for the weary. Not even for the dead.

He consoled his grieving friends with evanescent visits, rallied their drooping spirits, and fired their faith in a cemetery garden, on a country road, in an urban hideaway, on a mountain, and by the sea where they'd gone fishing to forget their woes. After he spent forty days posthumously putting his affairs in order, his Father called him home.

With his last steps on earth, he led his friends to Bethany (a place where *he* had called a man back from the grave) and left them his legacy: not land or jewels or money that would buy a leisured life, but a challenge, a daunting global mission, and a promise of power to carry it through.

The task was colossal, and it would cost most of them their lives, as it had cost him his. He said he'd be with them as a living Spirit, every hour of every day, somehow present even in his absence, sharing their toil, their pain, their joy, until time ends and eternity begins.

Then he was lifted into heaven, and he sat down beside God. His body healed, glorified, ascended. Yet his heart still earth-gripped and vulnerable. His ears reverberant with voices—pleading, anguished, despairing; faith-filled, doubting; desperate—echoing prayers he himself had sent Godward from riverbank and rocky plain, mountainside and olive garden, wilderness and skull-shaped hill, when he was mortal and in pain. He sat down beside God.

For a while.

How deeply can he rest, even on heaven's throne, when so few labor in his vineyard, and so great a harvest withers on the vine? There's work to be done in heaven, too. He prepares a place there for everyone who opens when he knocks and follows where he leads, who believes what he lived and died to tell us, and who bears the burden of love he bore. Cross bearers.

When all the places are ready and we've told the news to all creation—those who listen and those who won't—he'll return for love's last labor and bring each of his own to the place prepared, so that where he is—in paradise—we may be also.

The only happy ending that never ends.

The sparks fly upward.

Bibliography

The American Heritage Dictionary. New York: Dell, 2001.

Barth, Karl. *Dogmatics in Outline.* New York: Harper & Row, 1959.

Bryson, Bill. *A Short History of Nearly Everything.* New York: Broadway Books, 2003.

Burtt, E. A., ed., *The Teachings of the Compassionate Buddha.* New York: New American Library, 1955.

Catholic Encyclopedia. Vol. 1 and vol. 12. New York: Robert Appleton, 1907 and 1912.

Dawkins, Richard. *The God Delusion.* New York: Houghton Mifflin, 2006.

Dennett, Daniel C. *Breaking the Spell: Religion as a Natural Phenomenon.* New York: Penguin, 2006.

Dostoyevsky, Fyodor. *The Brothers Karamazov.* New York: New American Library, 1958.

Eaken, Emily. "So God's Really in the Details?" *New York Times.* May 11, 2002: B9.

Harris, Sam. *The End of Faith.* New York: W. W. Norton, 2004.

Haught, John F. *God and the New Atheism: A Critical Response to Dawkins, Harris, and Hitchens.* Louisville, KY: Westminster John Knox, 2008.

Hawking, Stephen, and Leonard Mlodinow. *The Grand Design.* New York: Bantam, 2010.

Hitchens, Christopher. *God Is Not Great: How Religion Poisons Everything.* New York: Hachette, 2007.

Isherwood, Christopher and Swami Prabhavananda, trans. *Baghavad-Gita: The Song of God.* New York: Mentor Books, 1959.

James, William. *The Varieties of Religious Experience.* New York: Modern Library, 1902.

Keats, John. "Letter to George and Georgiana Keats." *Selected Poems and Letters.* Ed. Douglas Bush. Boston: Houghton Mifflin, 1959. 283.

Lawrence, D. H. *Selected Poems.* New York: Viking, 1959.

Mascaro, Juan, trans. *The Upanishads.* London: Penguin, 1965.

Merton, Thomas. *New Seeds of Contemplation.* New York: New Directions, 1961.

—————. *Seeds of Contemplation*. Norfolk, CT: New Directions Books, 1949.

—————. *The Seven Storey Mountain*. New York: Harcourt, Brace, 1948.

—————. *Thoughts in Solitude*. New York: Farrar, Strauss and Cudahy, 1956.

—————. *The Waters of Siloe*. New York: Harcourt, Brace, 1949.

Nietzsche, Friedrich. *Beyond Good and Evil*. Chicago: Henry Regnery, 1955.

Patton, Laurie L., trans. *The Baghavad Gita*. London: Penguin Classics, 2008.

Peale, Norman Vincent. *Never Let Anything Get You Down (a sermon)*. Pawling, NY: Foundation for Christian Living, 1967.

Shorter Oxford English Dictionary. 5th ed. New York: Oxford University Press, 2002.

Simmons, Ernest J. *Leo Tolstoy*. New York: Vintage Books, 1960.

St. John of the Cross. *Dark Night of the Soul*. Mineola, NY: Dover, 2003.

Stenger, Victor J. *God: The Failed Hypothesis: How Science Shows that God Does Not Exist*. Amherst, NY: Prometheus Books, 2008.

Underhill, Evelyn. *Practical Mysticism*. New York: E. P. Dutton, 1960.

Walsh, James, trans. *The Cloud of Unknowing*. Mahwah, NJ: Paulist Press, 1981.

About the Author

A native Philadelphian, Shane Hayes earned his bachelor's and his law degrees from Villanova University, and studied for a year at Princeton Theological Seminary. He worked as a writer/editor for Prentice Hall and an attorney for the federal government. His personal essays have appeared in the *Saturday Evening Post*, the *Philadelphia Inquirer,* and other wide-circulation media. He is married, has four children, and lives in suburban Philadelphia. *Pretty Girl Lost* was his first novel. *The Last Dreamgirl* is his second, but the first to be published (Drake Valley Press, 2015).

His religious experience is multifaceted and gives him a rare perspective: he went from ardent Catholic (nearly a Trappist monk at seventeen), to militant atheist at twenty, to dilettante Hindu/Buddhist, to Pure Theist, to a Christian studying for the ministry at Princeton Theological Seminary, to a man with such strong ties to both Protestant and Catholic Christianity that he can identify himself only as "a Christian."

Colorful passages in Shane's life, all connected with writing or writers, were:

Meeting Merton: Meeting with Thomas Merton, the celebrated author, when Shane was seventeen and thinking of entering the Trappist monastery in Kentucky, where Merton was Master of Novices. Merton's profound influence on the youth, the boy's impressions of the man, and their conversation are recounted in *The End of Unbelief.*

Peale Power: Attending the Manhattan church at which Dr. Norman Vincent Peale, author of *The Power of Positive Thinking*, was pastor. Peale's eloquently proclaimed philosophy of positive thinking helped Shane survive years of adversity in his personal life. Peale quoted from one of Shane's newspaper articles in a speech to businessmen in Atlanta. In a letter, he told Shane he had done so, said the article was "terrific," and that a request had been made for reprints.

The Theroux You Never Knew: Ten days spent on a Greek ship sailing to New York from Piraeus with a new college grad named Paul Theroux, when he and Shane were in their early twenties, both brimming with literary ambition, unpublished, and unknown. Paul recently referred to that trip as "when my real life began." After an exchange of letters, they lost touch for forty years, while Paul became a famous author and a legendary traveler. When Shane reached out for a helping hand over that four decade chasm, Paul grasped it. He read, praised, and wrote endorsements for Shane's unpublished books.

White House Recognition: In 1971, Shane wrote several political pieces that caused a stir in Philadelphia newspapers. One came to the attention of then president Richard Nixon, who had his chief of staff Bob Haldeman call Shane to tell him the president had enjoyed the article and was passing it around to his staff. Haldeman invited Shane to the White House for lunch with head speechwriter Ray Price, who introduced him to prominent members of the president's staff: Haldeman, Colson, Buchanan, and Gergen.

Helping Holly: When Shane's daughter Holly was in high school, an English teacher required each student to have a parent explain reasons for imposing a certain kind of discipline on the